Genesis
Discovering God's
Answers to Life's
Ultimate
Questions

Bruce BICKEL
&
Stan JANTZ

HARVEST HOUSE™ PUBLISHERS

EUGENE, OREGON

All Scripture verses are taken from the *Holy Bible*, New Living Translation, copyright
©1996. Used by permission of Tyndale House Publishers, Inc., Wheaton, Illinois
60189, U.S.A. All rights reserved.

Cover by Left Coast Design, Portland, Oregon

Cover photo by Steve Terrill, Portland, Oregon, www.terrillphoto.com

Harvest House Publishers, Inc. is the exclusive licensee of the trademark, CHRISTIANITY
101.

GENESIS: DISCOVERING GOD'S ANSWERS TO LIFE'S ULTIMATE QUESTIONS
Copyright © 2003 by Bruce Bickel and Stan Jantz
Published by Harvest House Publishers
Eugene, Oregon 97402
www.harvesthousepublishers.com

Library of Congress Cataloging-in-Publication Data

Bickel, Bruce, 1952–
    Genesis: discovering God's answers to life's ultimate questions / Bruce Bickel and
Stan Jantz.
        p. cm. — (Christianity 101™)
    ISBN 0-7369-0793-9 (pbk.)
    1. Bible. O.T. Genesis—Commentaries. 2. Bible. O.T. Genesis—Study and teaching.
I. Jantz, Stan, 1952– II. Title. III. Series.
BS1235.53.B53 2003
222 ' . 1107—dc21   2002010765

All rights reserved. No part of this publication may be reproduced, stored in a retrieval
system, or transmitted in any form or by any means—electronic, mechanical, digital,
photocopy, recording, or any other—except for brief quotations in printed reviews,
without the prior permission of the publisher.

Printed in the United States of America

    03 04 05 06 07 08 09 10 11 / DP-KB / 10 9 8 7 6 5 4 3 2 1

Contents

The Beginning of God's Chosen People

A Note from the Authors

*I*f you can read only one book, then don't read this one. You are obviously interested in reading the Bible. You are particularly interested in reading Genesis (the first of 66 books contained in the Bible). If you can read only one book, set this one down and read Genesis.

The book you are holding in your hands is no substitute for Genesis. You've got to read the real thing. Our book may contain occasional outbursts of insight, but Genesis is divinely inspired from beginning to end. It is God's message to you. We can't compete with that. We aren't trying to.

Christianity 101 Bible Studies

This Bible study on Genesis is part of a series called *Christianity 101 Bible Studies*. Our goal for this study—and each one in the series—is simple. We want to give you a little help as you read through Genesis. We aren't going to bog things down with esoteric discussions of minor points of theology. And we promise not to take you on a tangent by conjugating Hebrew verbs. We are operating on the assumption that you want to read the Bible for yourself, but you can use a little help to keep you oriented along the way. Let's face it—the book of Genesis can be a little intimidating. At Genesis 1:1, the world doesn't even exist: In just 88 verses, you already have the world's first murder. You can get a sinus headache from traveling so fast. That's where we come in. We'll make sure you know the context of what you're reading.

Here is what we've got in store for you:

- In chapter 1, we'll give you an overview of the entire book of Genesis. If you were going to travel across the United States from San Francisco to New York, you'd look at the map first to see your route. You are more likely to enjoy the trip if you know exactly where you are at any point. That's why we are devoting the first chapter to the big picture. We'll identify themes that run throughout all of Genesis. If you know them ahead of time, they will be easier to spot as you come upon them in your reading.

- In chapters 2–13, we will take you on a passage-by-passage read through Genesis. We expect that your Bible will be open alongside this book. Read a chapter or two in Genesis, and then look to see what we've said about it. Or, you can read us first and then read the passage in Genesis. Either way works.

We won't spoon-feed you, but we'll make sure you get a "behind the scenes" perspective as you read. As with the other studies in this series, we're combining the biblical content of a commentary with the life applications of a Bible study. By reading this book and answering the questions at the end of each chapter, you will learn the basics of what you need to know to get more meaning from the Bible. Not only that, but you will be able to apply what the Bible says to your everyday Christian life. (This is particularly important with Genesis because in it you will find answers to some of the monumental questions that people ask about life.)

And just in case you want to go further with your study of Genesis, we've got a couple of bonus features for you:

- At the end of the book, in the Dig Deeper section, we've included a list of books and other material that you'll find helpful if you want more information.

- We've put together an online resource exclusively for the users of the Christianity 101 Bible Studies. To access this helpful tool and enhance your study of Genesis, visit www.christianity101online.com. (See page 153 for more details.)

This Book Is for You

Maybe you've never used a Bible resource before. Or maybe you're overwhelmed by the choices of resources available to you. Either way, we want to make sure that you are getting a book that will give you the kind of help you are looking for. So, just in case you are wondering, this book is for you if...

- You've never read the Bible before, and you are getting ready to start for the first time. You could go solo into Genesis, but we think you'll appreciate having two semi-talkative guides to give you a little color commentary along the way.

- You're experienced at reading the Bible, but every once in a while you get a little bored. Just as you might depend on a friend who makes sure you show up at the gym, you could use a couple of companions to supply some extra motivation to keep reading. We're glad to volunteer for the job. We promise to give you some background information and insights that we think you'll find pretty fascinating.

- You like reading the Bible, but you are not sure how it applies to real life. You don't know how to take what you read and translate it into your twenty-first-century lifestyle. Not to worry. God is just as relevant today as He was to Abraham back in 2000 B.C. The advent of indoor plumbing and computer technology make your circumstances different, but human nature and God's character haven't changed.

- You're interested in reading the Bible with a group of friends. Sort of like a book club that focuses on God's favorites. Everyone in your group will read through Genesis on their own, but this book can give direction to your group's discussions.

A Final Word Before We Begin

Genesis is filled with fascinating, true-life stories:

- You'll marvel at the account of how God created the universe by just speaking a few words.

- You'll blush as you see Adam and Eve attempt to conceal their nudity with a few strategically placed fig leaves.

- You'll wonder what Noah did with the woodpeckers on the ark.

But you'll miss the whole point of Genesis if you just read it for the stories. In the broad sense, Genesis is about God and His desire to have a relationship with humanity. But when you get down to specifics, Genesis is about God's desire to have a relationship with you. When you understand that, answers to most of your questions about life will become apparent. No one can answer your questions better than God Himself.

Chapter 1

Reading and studying Genesis are not burdensome tasks. Its themes are varied and its personal portraits unparalleled. It immediately tackles one of man's most basic questions: What is the origin of all things? Its answer is as credible as it is captivating.

—*John J. Davis*

*S*tart at the *B*eginning

Most people hate to walk into a movie theater after the film has started. They don't want to watch the movie unless they can catch it from the beginning. After all, you learn information at the start of the movie that helps explain things later on. If you miss the first part, the plot is more difficult to follow.

Reading the Bible is the same way. Oh sure, you can start anywhere, and it will make sense to you. But you'll have a much better idea of what is going on if you start at the beginning. God is introduced in the very first verse of the Bible, and humanity enters the picture 25 verses later. So if you want to know about the relationship between God and humanity in general—or God and you in particular—you might want to start at the beginning of the Bible. The plot will be easier to follow.

And that is why you are so perceptive and astute to be studying Genesis. You are getting in on the plot at the very beginning. In fact, that is what Genesis is all about: beginnings.

A Book of Beginnings

*W*hat's *A*head

- ☐ Part One of Five
- ☐ A Quick Overview
- ☐ Themes and Schemes

*T*he word *genesis* means "the origin" of something. It signifies the starting point or the beginning of a thing. So *Genesis* is an appropriate title for the first book of the Bible because in this book we learn of the beginning of all things.

Here are just a few of the "beginnings" and "firsts" that you'll find in Genesis:

- the first mention of God

- the beginning of the universe

- the beginning of the human race

- the first marriage (and the first time a husband tried to shift blame onto his wife)

- the first sin and the beginning of humanity's separation from God

- the first sacrifice

- the beginning of the family

- the first reference to a Messiah

- the beginning of civilizations, nations, and governments

- the beginning of the Jewish lineage

- the beginning of God's plan of salvation for humanity

From these beginnings, the plot of Genesis reveals some interesting progressions.

- You'll see humanity's origin in a perfect setting, and then you'll read about humanity's fall and constant spiritual struggle.

- You'll see God from a majestic cosmological point of view as He creates the universe, and then you'll read of His personal and intimate interaction with humans in one-to-one relationships.

- You'll see God's broad plan of redemption for all of humanity, and then you'll see how that plan plays out in the life of one man and his descendants.

For these reasons, Genesis may have more wide-reaching appeal than any other book of the Bible.

- It is of interest to scientists because it describes the origins of the universe.

- It is of interest to historians because it documents the beginning of society and the early history of Israel.

- It is of interest to theologians because it presents the nature and character of God.

- It is of interest to psychologists and sociologists because it deals with human nature.

But forget those other folks and their academic approach to Genesis. *You* will be fascinated by reading Genesis because it has personal relevance to you. In its 50 chapters, you will discover the answers to some of life's most perplexing questions:

- Where did you come from? (We are speaking cosmologically as well as biologically.)

- Why are you here?

- Why do you act the way that you do?

- Does life continue after death?

- Does God exist?

Don't expect to find these issues presented in a Q&A format. You'll find them embedded in the plot of the story that unfolds with each successive chapter.

Part One of Five

The Old Testament contains 39 books. Genesis is the first of them, but it is also considered as part of a group of the first five books (Genesis, Exodus, Leviticus, Numbers, and Deuteronomy). This group of five books is often referred to as the *Pentateuch,* from the Greek words *penta* (five) and *teuchos* (scroll or book).

Authorship: Moses or a Mosaic?

Nowhere in the book of Genesis does the author identify himself, but Moses is traditionally acknowledged to be its author. The book ends with the death of Joseph, which occurred approximately 300 years before Moses was born. Don't let that throw you. Oral tradition could account for the transfer of information down through the generations, but Moses wasn't relying on rumor or hearsay. The Bible tells us that the Holy Spirit divinely inspired its authors (2 Timothy 3:16). This explains the precise and accurate account. We can believe what Moses wrote about the creation of the world even though he wasn't around to see it when it happened.

Some scholars challenge the claim that Moses was the author of Genesis. They argue that Genesis is a compilation of writings collected over the centuries by a variety of authors. These scholars claim that Genesis is not a Mosaic work but rather a mosaic work of many ancient authors.

Perhaps more than any other person in the ancient world, Moses had the training and education necessary to write such a book. He grew up in Pharaoh's household and received a world-class education.

> *Moses was taught all the wisdom of the Egyptians, and he became mighty in both speech and action* (Acts 7:22).

God used the circumstances of Moses' life to help him comprehend all the available historical records and accounts of the origins and development of the world. And don't forget that he had the inspiration of the Holy Spirit.

But we don't need to merely speculate about Moses' authorship. Passages in the Pentateuch provide internal evidence that it was written by Moses. And other writings of the Old Testament attest that he was the author of the Pentateuch. Even the Roman historian Josephus declared authorship of the Pentateuch by Moses.

Who Is the Audience?

You are the audience as you read Genesis, but Moses probably didn't have you in mind when he wrote the book. Moses wrote Genesis and the rest of the Pentateuch for the Jews. This was their law. It established the principles for their understanding of God and their relationship with Him. You are not in the generation or the culture that Moses had in mind as he wrote Genesis, but the principles about God and humanity remain the same. The significance of the accounts recorded in Genesis may have nothing to do with your biological ancestors, but they are relevant to your spiritual heritage.

A Quick Overview

Genesis covers a broader time span than any other book of the Bible. It begins with Creation and ends with the death of Joseph (about 1800 B.C.). In chapter 2 of this book, we will see that arguments for the date of Creation range from 15 billion years ago to as recent as just 6000 B.C. Even using the most recent date, that makes the coverage of Genesis 4200 years. In contrast, the rest of the Old

Testament covers only 1100 years (from the birth of Moses in 1500 B.C. until about 400 B.C.). And the New Testament only covers about 100 years (from the birth of Christ until the end of the first century A.D. if you don't count the prophetic references of Revelation).

Genesis is a bit cumbersome, at least in terms of its time span. But we have several different ways to dissect it.

People and Events

Here is how Bruce Wilkinson and Kenneth Boa outline Genesis in their book *Talk Thru the Bible:*

A. Four Events Marking the Beginning of the Human Race

   1. Creation (1–2)

   2. The Fall (3–5)

   3. The Flood (6–9)

   4. Nations and the Tower of Babel (10:1–11:9)

B. Four People Marking the Beginning of the Hebrew Race

   1. Abraham (11:10–25:18)

   2. Isaac (25:19–26:35)

   3. Jacob (27–36)

   4. Joseph (37–50)

Places and Spaces

Another way to analyze the content of Genesis is to view it from a geographic perspective. In this context, the book divides nicely into three sections:

1. The Fertile Crescent (Genesis 1–11)

Humanity occupied Earth for several thousand years in the general vicinity of the Fertile Crescent. (This time period covers the events of the Garden of Eden, the flood, and the Tower of Babel.)

2. The Country of Canaan (Genesis 12–35)

In these chapters, the geographic scope of Genesis narrows to the land of Canaan, which God promised to give to Abraham and his descendants. This part of the story line focuses on Abraham, Isaac, and Jacob.

3. Egypt (Genesis 36–50)

In the last part of Genesis, the descendants of Abraham are on the verge of extinction. But God's plan includes routing Joseph into Egypt, and in that country the fledgling tribe of Hebrews finds a temporary home.

All About Beginnings

We've got 50 chapters of Genesis to cover in chapters 2–13 of this book. No matter how you do the math, that is a lot of ground (and time) to cover. But in the next 12 chapters of this book, we will dissect Genesis into these three sections:

Chapters 2–6: The Beginning of the World (Genesis 1–11)

In this section, we'll start at Creation and go through the Tower of Babel. That covers the origin of the universe, the beginning of humanity, and the beginnings of civilization.

Chapters 7–10: The Beginning of God's Covenant (Genesis 12–20)

Genesis 12 marks a shift in focus from civilization down to one man: Abraham. God made certain promises (covenants) to Abraham. These covenants serve as the basis for God's plan to rescue humanity from its terrible plight.

Chapters 11–13: The Beginning of God's Chosen People (Genesis 21–50)

God's "chosen people" are the descendants of Abraham. The first was Abraham's son, Isaac, whose story begins in Genesis 21. The family tree continues as it expands through the rest of Genesis.

Themes and Schemes

Genesis is full of themes that keep reoccurring in the story line. But these themes don't end at the conclusion of Genesis. They continue through the rest of the Bible. The New Testament emphasizes and amplifies many of the themes that Genesis presents. Some of the themes describe the character traits of God. As you might expect, His personality is consistent throughout Genesis (and the rest of Scripture). Some of the other themes focus on the sinful schemes of humanity (which are also consistent).

We'll highlight the major themes of Genesis in the following chapters of this book. For now, we'll give you a "heads up" for what you should be looking for.

A God-Centered Worldview

Genesis presents the existence of God without equivocation. God exists, and He created everything else by His power. Genesis presents God as the sole and sovereign Ruler of the universe. He is the Creator and Sustainer of all life.

If you analyze the character traits of God that Genesis presents, you will come to these undeniable conclusions:

- God is *personal*—He desires a relationship with each individual.

- God is *loving*—He is a God who wants what is best for us.

- God is *just*—He cannot tolerate sin.

- God is *forgiving*—He will make a way to rescue us from the power and penalty of sin so that our relationship with Him can be restored.

Genesis presents a picture of the one and only God. The concept of a monotheistic (one-God) religion probably doesn't catch you by surprise, but it was contrary to what the ancient cultures believed.

	According to Genesis	According to the Egyptians	According to the Greeks
Concept of God	One God	Many gods and goddesses	Many gods and goddesses *(in combat with each other)*
Characteristics of God	All-powerful, self-existent	Representative of nature and abstract ideas	Adulterous, mischievous, immature
God's Relationship with Humanity	Desires a personal relationship with each individual	Operate independent of any connection with humanity	Intervene in lives of humans for sport and spite

The Nature of Humanity

According to Genesis, humanity is not merely a random, chance happening of the evolutionary cycle. God specifically and purposefully designed us.

- *We are created in God's image.* This means that we have an eternal, spiritual dimension to our lives. It is the "soul" part of us, which has eternal existence.

- *We have a free will.* God could have created us as robots to do His bidding, but He gave us the ability to make choices.

- *Without God's intervention, we would be doomed.* The track record of humanity is not good. Beginning with Adam, humanity has chosen to rebel against God, and we've continued in a downward spiral of immorality, pride, and selfishness.

Blessings and Curses

The formula is simple. If you follow God's principles, you will realize His blessings in your life. Conversely, if you disobey His precepts, you'll bring trouble and hardship on yourself.

An Example to the World

God promised Abraham that his descendants would display God's principles to the world. Through the "Children of Israel," God would demonstrate that obedience brings blessings and disobedience brings hardship. Abraham and his descendants lived out both truths. Their lives were sometimes blessed by God and sometimes cursed as they waffled between obedience and rebellion.

God hasn't suspended these principles. They still apply today. And you will be proof of the principles in one way or another. Imagine that someone is objectively observing your life to determine the pros and cons of obedience to God's principles. What does your life reveal? Are you being faithful to Him? Or are you acting like He doesn't exist? What blessings of God do you experience when you obey His principles? What is your life like when you live in rebellion?

A Plan of Salvation

We've saved the best theme for last. Most people are aware that the crucifixion of Christ was part of God's plan for our salvation. Not everyone realizes that plan was revealed in Genesis. Before Adam's sin, God laid the groundwork for humanity's salvation. The work of Christ on the cross is foreshadowed in Genesis with the symbolism of the sacrificial offerings.

■ ■ ■

Study the Word

1. Check out these references for statements in the Pentateuch about its authorship: Exodus 17:14; Leviticus 1:1-2; Numbers 33:2; Deuteronomy 1:1.

2. What was Christ's opinion about the authorship of the Pentateuch? See Matthew 8:4; Mark 12:26; Luke 16:29; John 7:19.

3. Find a map that covers the regions mentioned in Genesis. Identify the three geographic places that are central to the story line of Genesis: the Fertile Crescent, Canaan, and Egypt.

4. What are the implications of a worldview that is centered on a sovereign God?

5. What are the implications of a worldview that excludes God?

6. Read Psalm 104; Psalm 148; and Isaiah 40. How should we respond to God as our Creator?

The Beginning of the World

Chapter 2

It seems to me that when confronted with
the marvels of life and the universe one
must ask why and not just how.

—*Professor Arthur L. Schawlow,*
Stanford University

The Great Debate

Skip this chapter if controversy makes you squeamish. God apparently isn't bothered by controversy because He begins the Bible with one of the most hotly contested and debated issues in our society. Genesis 1 (and parts of Genesis 2) are all about the great Creation vs. Evolution debate. As you can imagine, these chapters are the basis of argument between the followers of Christ and the followers of Darwin. If you have been afraid to enter the debate because you believe the Bible but think that science is stacked against you, then we've got a few surprises for you in the pages that follow.

We'll get into a little bit of science in this chapter, but you won't need a lab coat or a pocket protector. The debate can be simplified to a simple question: God or no God? That's the bottom line. The issue doesn't have to get any more complicated than that.

How It All Began

Genesis 1

*Y*ou probably refer to God by many different names: Lord, Heavenly Father, or God Almighty. Well, we've got another name for God that is derived from the very first verse in the Bible. God is "the First Big Cause."

Moses didn't waste any time before identifying God's role in the universe. Right there in Genesis 1:1, he states, "In the beginning, God created the heavens and the earth."

Don't let the apparent simplicity of this verse fool you. The implications are huge.

The First Big Cause

Genesis 1:1 presents an insurmountable argument against the claim that a belief in God goes against logic

27

and reason. Genesis 1:1 is all about logical thinking. In fact, this verse is a good illustration of the principle of cause and effect that states, Every effect has a cause. In Genesis 1:1, the creation of the universe was the effect, and God was the cause.

But don't take our word for it. Decide for yourself. If this principle isn't true, then we are left with only three possibilities about the universe:

Option 1: The universe doesn't exist. This is an option in theory, but it doesn't remain an option in reality. After all, you are here. You and the chair you are sitting on are tangible. Things exist. So option 1 is out.

Option 2: The universe has always existed. This concept is not as far-fetched as option 1. For many years, scientists believed that the universe had always existed in a "steady state." They believed it didn't need a cause to get it going because it always was. But during the last century, scientists made discoveries in astronomy, physics, and chemistry that proved the "steady state" theory to be erroneous. When the Cosmic Background Explorer satellite confirmed the Big Bang, scientists had incontrovertible proof that the universe had a point of beginning. The Big Bang disproved option 2.

Option 3: The universe created itself. We can quickly rule this option out. Logic and reason dictate that things don't create themselves. This principle is so entrenched in the logic lexicon that it has its own Latin descriptive phrase: *Ex nihilo nihil fit.*

If you are a little rusty on your Latin, allow us to remind you of the English translation: "From nothing, nothing comes." Our personal translation is a little more casual but nonetheless accurate: "You don't get something from nothing."

Having ruled out options 1, 2, and 3, we are left with the only possibility:

Option 4: Some independent outside force must have caused the universe to come into existence. This gets us back to where we started. The universe exists, so some cause must have produced it.

God is the only possible cause that could have created the universe. Anything else would be a part of the universe, and we know that a thing can't create itself (or have you so soon forgotten the fallacy of option 3?).

Why is this issue of cause and effect so important to a study of Genesis? We're glad you asked. We can confirm aspects of God's character when we know that He was the First Big Cause who created the universe.

Science writer Fred Hereen interviewed the leading scientists of our age (including the likes of Stephen Hawking, Nobel prize winners, and NASA researchers). In response to their findings and comments, Hereen has identified six features that must be true about the first cause that produced the universe. Because God was the First Big Cause, these six features are true about Him.

1. The first cause must be independent of the universe.

As we discussed above, since the universe can't create itself, the first cause must be outside of the universe. This feature describes the *transcendent* nature of God—He transcends the universe. He is above and beyond it. It is subject to His control. See Hebrews 1:10-12.

2. The first cause must be all-powerful.

Scientists describe the Big Bang as the greatest explosion of energy that has ever occurred in the universe. The first cause would have to have the power to create that explosion. And that is exactly how the Bible describes

God when it speaks of His *omnipotence* (all-powerfulness). See Jeremiah 32:17.

3. The first cause must be timeless.

Because the first cause must be outside our universe, it must be beyond our parameters of time. It must have pre-existed the start of the universe. This feature is consistent with God's eternal (timeless) nature. See Psalm 90:2.

4. The first cause must be supernatural.

Just as the first cause is outside of time, it must also be outside the physical realm. It transcended the physical realm before the physical universe existed. God fits this description because He is a spirit. He is not composed of matter and does not possess a physical nature. See John 4:24.

5. This first cause must be a supreme intelligence.

To put the incredible complexity of the universe into place, the first cause must have the knowledge that encompasses and surpasses all of it. Albert Einstein said that the intellect of the first cause "reveals an intelligence of such superiority that, compared with it, all the systematic thinking and acting of human beings is an utterly insignificant reflection." That description fits God. He is *omniscient* (all-knowing) and has knowledge of all the laws of nature because He put them into place. See Psalm 147:5.

6. The first cause must have a personality.

This trait refers to the fact that the first cause must have acted intentionally—on purpose—with a particular result in mind. Hereen cites prominent scientists who find evidence of purpose and intention behind the intelligent life in the universe. God has such a personality. He is not some amorphous force. He is a personal God with a will and a purpose. (See Psalm 94:9-10.)

We should not be surprised that God fits perfectly into the profile of the first cause described by Hereen. After all, Genesis 1:1 tells us that God was the First Big Cause (although it doesn't use that contemporary scientific reference). From about 1450 B.C., when Moses wrote Genesis, the Bible has been declaring that God created the universe. Now, about 3500 years later, the profile of the first cause confirms what the Bible has been saying all along.

So Where Did God Come From?

Genesis 1 explains how everything in the universe began. Well, that's not exactly correct. It doesn't explain where God came from.

Genesis 1:1 says that God was around "in the beginning." That verse presupposes that God existed even before things began (and that's how He happened to be there at the beginning). This verse means that God had no beginning. He always existed. He didn't create Himself. He is the one and only self-existent Being.

For every house has a builder, but God is the one who made everything (Hebrews 3:4).

A Six-Day Work Week

Moses describes the formation of the universe and all of its contents as happening in six distinct steps. These are the six "days" of Creation.

Day 1: God gets a Big Bang out of Creation (1:1-5).

God existed, but the universe did not. Then, at God's command, the universe came into existence, complete with planet Earth in its own solar system (including the sun by day and the moon by night). Scientists have determined that the universe had a definite point of beginning. They call it the Big Bang, but we suspect that the sound was much bigger than *bang* when God said, "Let there be light."

As you read the first five verses of Genesis 1, notice that the perspective seems to be from outer space, as if God were looking down from heaven on what is happening below. When you get to day 2 and following, the perspective is from Earth (as if you were looking up into the sky).

Moses would naturally shift the perspective in this manner. After all, he wasn't writing a scientific textbook. He was intent on telling the story of the relationship between God and mankind. So after dealing with outer space (day 1), he quickly turned his attention back to Earth (days 2 through 6).

Day 2: Water evaporates into thin air (1:6-8).

Next, God got the evaporation cycle going. Day 1 left Earth with a murky atmosphere, but the combination of sunlight and evaporation put clouds in the sky. On a grand scale, the evaporation caused the water on Earth's surface to recede as rain clouds formed.

Day 3: Earth becomes a seedy place (1:9-13).

As the water on Earth receded on day 2, the ground appeared. With the cloudy atmosphere and all that evaporation, Earth was like a giant greenhouse. Since God knew all about botany (remember that omniscience characteristic), He knew this would be a perfect growing climate for plants. So now was a good time to create them.

Day 4: On a clear day, you can see forever (1:14-19).

The plants started growing, and you know what that means—photosynthesis. (Or have you forgotten that display board you made for your fifth-grade science fair?) The production of oxygen from the plants cleared up the atmosphere. The sky changed from murky to transparent. For the first time, the sun, moon, and stars became clearly visible from Earth.

God didn't create the sun, moon, and stars on day 4. (That had already happened in day 1.) But the atmosphere cleared up in day 4 so that they became apparent for the first time from the perspective of an observer on Earth.

Day 5: Fish gotta swim and birds gotta fly (1:20-23).

Having created all of those oceans and all of that clear sky, God then created swimmers and flyers to occupy those regions.

Day 6: Lions and tigers and Adam and Eve (1:24-31).

Let's review. God grew vegetables (day 3), and He had fish and poultry (day 5). But God knew that you can't have a really successful restaurant without beef on the menu. So on day 6, He created wild animals and livestock. And then only one thing was missing. Have you noticed what it is? You! (Well, not you exactly, but your ancestors.) Fortunately for you (and us), God completed the work on day 6 with the creation of man and woman.

What Does Science Say?

Science is not God's enemy. After all, God invented science. Of course, some scientists want to deny the existence of God, but they are finding that much more difficult to do in light of the continuing discoveries in astronomy, astrophysics, and microbiology. A growing number of scientists, including some who are non-Christians and agnostics, conclude that the universe and the human body could not have just happened. Everything about the complexities of our galaxies and functioning of our bodies is so finely tuned that some intelligent designer must have put it into place. Not surprisingly, these scientists subscribe to the "Intelligent Design" theory of the universe. They are winning the debate with scientists who adhere to Darwin's theory that the universe exists by accident and evolution.

We'll talk more about evolution in the next section. But before you put your test tube and Bunsen burner away, we thought you'd like to see what scientists (including Darwinists) have determined to be the sequence of Earth's development. We'll even compare science's sequence with the progression described by Moses. Don't worry that technology gives modern science an unfair advantage over Moses, who made his pronouncements about 3500 years ago. Remember that Moses had a little help from God to explain what happened.

The Sequence According to Moses	The Sequence According to Science
Day 1—Heavens and Earth are created	The Big Bang
Day 2—Waters separate	Earth's atmosphere changes
Day 3—Dry land appears	Bacteria and algae plant life begin to grow
Day 4—Sun, moon, and stars are visible	Earth's atmosphere becomes transparent
Day 5—First animal life in water and air	Molecular life in water, winged insects in air
Day 6—Land animals created, followed by humans	Land animals appear, humans appear later

The sequence in Genesis matches the sequence determined by science. (God must be relieved that He is finally validated and verified.) Of course, we don't look to science to prove God exists. We can confidently put our faith in God because of who He is. Sometimes it takes science a little time to catch up.

The Daze Surrounding the Days

The Bible clearly states *who* was responsible for creation: God. And we even know *how* He created it: He just said the words and things came into being (see Genesis 1:3,6,9,11,14,20,24,26). But the Bible isn't specific about the *when* of creation.

Even the Hebrew phrase *in the beginning* is a little ambiguous. It doesn't always mean "at the very first moment." Sometimes it can refer to the beginning stages or phases. Old Testament scholar and Hebrew language expert John Sailhamer writes:

> Since the Hebrew word translated "beginning" refers to an indefinite period of time, we cannot say for certain when God created the world or how long He took to create it. This period could have spanned as much as several billion years, or it could have been much less; the text simply does not tell us how long. It tells us only that God did it during the "beginning" of our universe's history.

Even more mystery (and controversy) surrounds the meaning of the word *day* as used in Genesis 1. Just as the word *day* can have different meanings in English, so it has three different meanings in Hebrew that indicate three different periods of time:

Sunrise to sunset. The Hebrew word for "day" in Genesis 1 can refer to a 12-hour period of time. We use the same meaning in English when we say, "I worked all day." We aren't saying that we worked for 24 hours; we just mean that we put in a full workday of approximately eight hours.

Sunset to sunset. The Hebrew word can also refer to a 24-hour period of time. This would be the same as if you said, "My birthday is in three days."

A long period of time unrelated to the sun. Here the Hebrew word for "day" can refer to anything from a few weeks to a year or even an age. Again, our English word *day* can have this same meaning. Have you ever heard an old person say, "In my day we had to walk two miles to school in the snow, and we were barefoot"? You get the idea.

Two Interpretations of Timing

There are two major, opposing points of view about the timing of the Creation events. But before we describe them to you, we want to emphasize that both views hold the following "essential" beliefs:

- God created the universe.

- The Bible is the completely true Word of God.

- Our knowledge of God and His ways is incomplete.

View 1: The "Young Earth" View

This is the view that God created the universe approximately 6000 to 10,000 years ago in a period of six literal 24-hour days. The reason Earth looks much older to geologists can be explained primarily by Noah's global flood

(Genesis 6–8), which dramatically changed the geology of Earth. For example, rather than being formed over millions of years through gradual erosion, the Grand Canyon was formed in a period of weeks or months by the rapid and powerful receding waters of Noah's flood.

As for the measurement of light that would seem to indicate an older universe, young-Earth creationists claim the speed of light was much faster just after Creation than it is now. This means that light from distant galaxies got here right away rather than over a period of billions of years.

Young-Earth creationists interpret the Creation account in Genesis literally. They prefer a "probable" reading of the Bible—in other words, take it for what it says—even if it contradicts a more "plausible" scientific picture of an older Earth. Furthermore, science is always changing. What we believe to be true today may not be true tomorrow (remember that scientists once claimed the world was flat).

View 2: The "Old Earth" View

Also known as "progressive" creationism, this view teaches that God created the universe 10 to 15 billion years ago. Some old-Earth creationists believe the "days" of Creation in Genesis are long periods of time (a "day-age" view), while others believe that each "day" of Creation was a literal 24-hour day separated by long periods of time (a "gap" or "intermittent-day" view).

While the Bible doesn't give us the age of the Earth or the universe, it does tell us that God doesn't operate under the same time dimension that envelops man. Furthermore, the scientific evidence seems to point more and more to a universe that is billions and billions of years old. Old-Earth creationists cite light as an example.

Because the light we see from stars has traveled across space at a rate of 186,000 miles per second, astronomers measure the distance light travels in light-years. The most distant galaxies are 10 billion light-years away, which means that the universe is at least 10 billion years old.

■ ▦ ▨

$\mathcal{S}$tudy the $\mathcal{W}$ord

1. Genesis 1:1–2:3 presents the account of the creation of the world from a global perspective. Genesis 2:4-25 retells the account from a much more personal perspective. For a poetic version of the creation account as told by King David, read Psalm 104.

2. Read Psalm 90:4 (written by Moses) and 1 John 2:18. How do these verses relate to the "young Earth vs. old Earth" debate?

3. The Trinity is the three Persons of God: the Father, the Son, and the Holy Spirit. All three Persons of the Trinity were involved in Creation. Look in Genesis 1 for "us" references to God.

4. Read John 1:1-14; Colossians 1:15-17; and Hebrews 1:1-4,10-12. What do these verses teach about Christ's involvement in the creation process?

5. What does the creation of the world reveal to us about the nature and character of God?

Chapter 3

This narrative addresses the most troubling question faced by every human: "Why must I die?" In addition it gives a reason for several fundamental features of human experience—wearing clothes, pain in childbirth...and the enmity between humans and snakes. Much more importantly, this simple account offers penetrating insight into...the deep tensions between husband and wife and between humans and God.

—*John E. Hartley*

What a Pace

You've only read one chapter in the Bible, and we've already covered the entire cosmos. What's left? Well, now Moses narrows the focus a bit. But keep your seatbelt fastened because the pace doesn't slow down very much.

You're going to be exhausted after you read the next ten chapters of Genesis. You won't strain your eyes because you'll only read 266 verses. But you might blow your mind and drain your emotions. The action, adventure, and drama never stop. (Maybe Moses was sensitive to this fact. He slowed the pace down with some mellow genealogies in chapters 5, 10, and 11.)

You're the Only One for Me

Genesis 2

The creation of humanity was reported in Genesis 1, but now the story repeats a bit—this time getting much more personal. We learn the names of the first man and woman, and we learn how they met. They have a bit of a romantic encounter. Actually, they had an arranged marriage, but maybe that is what makes it so romantic. God designed Adam and Eve for each other.

The Bible doesn't say how long Adam and Eve lived in the Garden of Eden before they sinned and God kicked them out (which you'll read about in Genesis 3). We think they lived there for quite a while and were very happy (which made their eviction from the Garden even worse). We can just imagine the two of them sitting on a grassy slope as they enjoy the scenery and a summer breeze. In a romantic and reflective moment, Eve asks,

"Adam, do you love me?" To which he responds with typical male callousness, "Who else?"

In reality, the life and romance of Adam and Eve is quite a story. But before you get to it, Genesis 2 repeats the entire Creation sequence (2:4-7). This is not a second Creation. Genesis 2 provides a review before it gives new information. Think about describing a summer vacation to a friend. You might say where you went and the highlights of what you did. Then, when you think of a particular episode you want to describe, you might repeat a few of the details to put the specific incident into the proper context. That is what happens in Genesis. Chapter 1 gives the broad overview of all of Creation. Chapter 2 returns to focus on the creation of the human race with more detail.

You Can't Get to Eden from Here

Eden was located at the apex of four rivers, two of which are known today as the Tigris and Euphrates. They originate in Armenia. The other two rivers cannot be located, and any trace of them may be obliterated by topographical changes.

Eden was located in the region known as the Fertile Crescent. Not surprisingly, this is the area where the earliest records of civilization have been found.

The world before the time of Noah's flood was quite different from the world that we know. Heavy cloud cover filtered the sunlight. Instead of rain, heavy mists in the morning and evening watered the vegetation. The Garden of Eden was unlike anything we can imagine. But the Bible gives us a few clues to what it was like:

- Natural beauty enhanced Adam and Eve's creativity and relaxation.

- Adam and Eve received meaningful work assignments and were productive.

- They undoubtedly took time for recreation.

- The design of the Garden fostered companionship.

- Adam and Eve enjoyed a close, intimate relationship with God.

Some people have complained that the placement of the "tree of the knowledge of good and evil" in the middle of the Garden was some sort of trap. It was no such thing. God gave clear and specific instruction to Adam to stay away from it. Rather than a trap, the placement of the tree was an opportunity for man to display his character (as either obedient or disobedient).

In the Image of God

What does being created in "the image of God" mean? Well, it definitely doesn't mean that God has a nose and His second toe on each foot is slightly longer than each big toe.

When the Bible speaks of God creating humanity in His own image, it is referring to moral, spiritual, and eternal qualities instead of physical characteristics. When God breathed life into Adam, he and all of the members of the human race to follow received capacities that God has. Like God, we have an eternal nature (our soul). And we possess the ability to think, feel, and reason. We have a sense of morality and a conscience. And we have a free will for making decisions. Unlike the animals, we have the capacity to enjoy fellowship with God. Any good part of our being can be explained by our origins: We were made in God's image.

Our creation in the image of God precludes evolution as Darwin theorized. Yes, *microevolution* does occur within a species (some characteristics of a species can change slightly over time). But no one has proved that *macroevolution*—one species changing into another (like a wiener dog morphing into an alligator)—has ever occurred. No one has found the infamous "missing link" (although there have been a few hoaxes). And the fossil record shows absolutely none of the transitional life forms that Darwin predicted we would find. God specifically and specially created the human race.

What a Woman

At the time Moses was writing Genesis, the culture was very patriarchal (father-centered). That male-dominated aspect of society continued for many centuries and still exists in many regions and cultures. But it was particularly prevalent in Old Testament times. Women were second-class citizens of society. They had little influence outside the home, and inside the house they were subservient to "the man of the house" (although in Israel they had more rights and received more respect than in other ancient societies).

This never has been God's opinion of women. Genesis 2 stands as a clear proclamation of God's view of the prominence, competence, and importance of women. In fact, this passage in Genesis emphasizes the similarities of Adam and Eve rather than their differences. God created women to have worth, value, and respect. God makes no distinction in such regards between men and women.

Eve, as the first member of the feminine sisterhood, claimed these distinctions for her gender:

- God created her in His own image.

- God gave her a full share in humanity's dominion over the animals.

God intended Adam and Eve to be equal partners. As you'll read in the next section, sin ruined the balance and God restructured the husband/wife relationship. While equality of worth remains, the husband has received a leadership role in the family. (This leadership certainly isn't based on any shred of supposed male superiority. It is simply a chain-of-authority organizational feature instituted by God.)

Marriage Is God's Idea

We can learn important principles about marriage from the relationship between Adam and Eve that God structured.

1. Marriage is a divinely designed relationship.

It was instituted by God as His idea from the outset. (It was also an arranged marriage, but that point is a bit irrelevant since neither Adam or Eve had other options.)

2. Marriage is a monogamous relationship.

God selected one wife for Adam, not several of them. Furthermore, God expected sexual fidelity in marriage. The "united as one" reference in Genesis 2:24 is more than just a figurative phrase to be used at weddings.

3. Marriage is a heterosexual relationship.

The first marriage set the pattern. While friendship and loyalty can exist between people of the same gender, God designed marriage for a man and a woman.

4. Marriage is a unified relationship.

The husband and wife are connected to each other emotionally, physically, and spiritually. By these bonds, they are "one."

5. *Marriage is a permanent relationship.*

The unity of marriage implies the permanency of marriage. Divorce is not part of God's ideal plan.

But What About All of Those Wives?

The Old Testament is filled with examples of men who had many wives. Some of these guys were supposedly great men of God (like King David) or supposedly very wise (like King Solomon). If marriage is supposed to be a one-husband/one-wife relationship, why do we see so much polygamy in the Old Testament?

Polygamy was very common in ancient cultures of the Middle East. It happened, but God didn't authorize it, nor did He like it. The same is true of divorce. As Jesus said in discussing this subject, "It was not what God had originally intended" (Matthew 19:8).

■ ■ ■

Study the Word

1. King David was a student of human nature. Read what he wrote in Psalm 8 about the nature of mankind. What does that add to your understanding of the image of God in you?

2. The image of God gives us value and infinite worth.
    Read Hebrews 2:5-18. What does this passage tell you
    about yourself?

3. To get a better understanding of the value and con-
    tribution of women (even in Bible times), read
    Proverbs 31. How do those descriptions of the
    woman's activities translate into contemporary
    society?

4. Adam and Eve didn't have problems with in-laws, but
    maybe you do. A person's loyalty to parents can
    sometimes conflict with the commitment to a spouse.
    What guidelines has God established for dealing with
    this conflict if it arises? (See Genesis 2:24; see also
    Exodus 20:12.)

Chapter 4

This passage provides the answer to another of the big questions of life: How do we account for the origin of sin and evil in the world? The Genesis record makes it clear that sin was not a part of God's original creation. Rather, it came as the result of the temptation of the first human pair, whom God had created with the power of choice. Man freely chose to rebel against God at the suggestion of an alien evil spirit.

—Howard F. Vos

Don't Think That You Know It All

You are about to read some stories you are familiar with. Here in Genesis 3 you'll find Adam and Eve and the snake, and later come the accounts of Cain and Abel (Genesis 4), Noah's flood (Genesis 6), and the Tower of Babel (Genesis 11). These may be very familiar stories for you, but don't think that you can skip over them. If you read them carefully, you'll gain great insights about God and yourself.

Genesis 3 is a great example of this. Have you ever wondered why so often you naturally want to do the wrong thing? And why is doing the right thing sometimes so difficult? Don't blame our culture. Our dark side is more inbred than that. Just ask any parent of a toddler. Disobedience comes easily for those little children.

So don't drift off as you read the familiar story of Adam and Eve and the apple. If you read it carefully, you might learn some new facts. (For example, the Bible never says that the forbidden fruit was an apple.) More importantly, you might learn something about yourself.

Sin and the Downfall

Genesis 3

*W*hen we last saw Adam and Eve (in Genesis 2), they were living in beautiful tranquility. All was well with them and the world. They had a relatively stress-free life. All they had to remember was to not eat the fruit from the "tree of the knowledge of good and evil" (Genesis 2:17). That seems simple enough, doesn't it?

Behavior isn't so simple, however, when temptation is involved. When given the notion to choose, Adam and Eve made the wrong choice.

A Strategy for Temptation

We do well to examine how Satan tempted Eve (Genesis 3:1-5) because he uses the same techniques today. Look at this progression:

- God laid down the rules. They were simple and clear: Don't eat the fruit from one particular tree. (See 2:16-17.) Even though God gave this command to Adam, Eve knew the rule.

- Satan presented a question that misstated God's rule. "Did God *really* say you must not eat *any* of the fruit in the garden?"

- Then Satan disputes what God has said. Eve: "God says we must not eat it or even touch it, or we will die." Satan: "You won't die!"

- Then Satan adds a few lies to further obscure the difference between right and wrong. "You will become just like God."

That's how Satan operates. He gets us to question God, and then we doubt what God has said. If we keep thinking that way, we will end up denying the truth of what God has said. Denial results in our disobedience.

Satan is the master of making a bad thing look good. And that's how Adam fell (without any prolonged personal tempting by Satan). The forbidden fruit "looked so fresh and delicious" to him, and Eve was probably giving it culinary kudos.

Sometimes, like Eve, we slip into sin because we aren't thinking straight. Other times, like Adam, we make an affirmative, intentional decision to sin simply because we want the momentary pleasure that a bad thing offers.

Sin Brings Consequences

The effects of the sin that day in the Garden of Eden were far-reaching. The consequences of the sin of Adam and Eve extend to all the males and females who follow them in the human family.

- Life is hard. Instead of a supervisory position in the Garden of Eden, Adam is sentenced to a life of hard labor.

- Eve is also sentenced to a life of hard labor but in the context of childbirth. When God had told them (in 1:28) to "multiply and fill the earth," that must have sounded like a fun activity. Now pain is associated with it.

- The ideal and tranquil cooperative partnership between Adam and Eve is readjusted. Male leadership is a sore point.

- Death comes to Adam and Eve as the ultimate punishment. This applies to physical death ("to the dust you will return"), which apparently wasn't a factor until their sin.

The consequences of the sin of Adam and Eve are so horrendous for all of humanity that their sin is often referred to as "the fall." By their acts, sin entered the world. They contracted a contagious disease (the sin virus) that would infect all of their descendants for all generations.

> *When Adam sinned, sin entered the entire human race. Adam's sin brought death, so death spread to everyone, for everyone sinned* (Romans 5:12).

Our sin nature, which we inherited from Adam, brings spiritual death (Romans 6:23) as well as physical death. Although physical death is bad, spiritual death is worse because it lasts for eternity and involves everlasting punishment and separation from God.

But don't despair. Christ is the cure for the sin virus.

> *What a contrast between Adam and Christ, who was yet to come! And what a difference between our sin and God's generous gift of forgiveness. For this one man, Adam, brought death to many through his sin. But this other man, Jesus Christ, brought forgiveness to many through God's bountiful gift!... The sin of this one man, Adam, caused death to rule over us, but all who receive God's wonderful, gracious gift of righteousness will live in triumph over sin and death through this one man, Jesus Christ* (Romans 5:14-17).

The Psychological Effects of Sin

This is a great passage for identifying the psychological impact of sin. In 3:8-13, look at the mental and emotional toll that sin took on Adam and Eve:

- They were riddled with guilt.
- They hid from God, isolating themselves from the One who loved them.
- They were afraid of God.
- They were ashamed of themselves.
- They started arguing and blaming each other.

Sin will rob you of mental and emotional stability. Your natural reaction will be to run from God. Don't do it. That's exactly the time when you need to return to God and ask His forgiveness.

If You Look Hard, You Can See Jesus

Are you surprised that after only a few pages of the Bible you're already finding references to Jesus? (And you thought He didn't show up until the New Testament.) Of course, He isn't mentioned by name, so you have to pay attention, or you'll skip right over Him.

"He will crush your head, and you will strike his heel." God recited this rather strange punishment on Satan in Genesis 3:15 when He referred to the offspring of Eve. It is a reference to Jesus Christ (who was the offspring of Eve, many generations later). "You will strike his heel" refers to the attempts that Satan instigated to defeat Christ during His life on Earth. "He will crush your head" describes Christ's triumph over Satan when Jesus rose from the dead after His crucifixion. That single act destroyed Satan's schemes to thwart God's plan of providing salvation to the human race.

At the end of chapter 3, God made coverings for Adam and Eve out of animal skins to replace the flimsy fig leaves (3:21). Moses does not mention an animal sacrifice on an altar, but he must have known that the Hebrew people would have that mental image as they read this verse. Animal sacrifices were a regular part of worship for the Jews. The blood of an innocent animal symbolically represented God's forgiveness of their sins. God probably didn't perform a sacrificial ceremony there in the Garden of Eden, but Adam and Eve may have seen the death of the innocent animals. They might have been shocked by the high cost of their sin. Something innocent had to die to provide a covering for sin.

Both of these verses present a picture of the work of Christ on the cross. Although He was innocent, He gave

His life. His crucifixion crushed Satan's schemes. His blood was the covering for our sins.

◾ ◾ ◾

Study the Word

1. Satan brought temptation into the Garden of Eden. But his evil existed before Adam and Eve. Read Isaiah 14:12-14 to get a "behind the scenes" view of Satan's expulsion from heaven. What are some similarities between Satan's attitude in Isaiah 14:13-14 and his approach to Eve in the Garden?

2. What were Eve's weaknesses? In what way did Satan's temptation appeal to her? How about you? If you were in the Garden, what weaknesses would Satan try to exploit, and how do you think he would go about it? In what ways does Satan try to tempt you into sin here and now?

3. Give a definition of sin based on Genesis 3. Adam and Eve obviously knew they were disobeying God, but do you think they thought in advance about the consequences? Do the sins in your life creep up unexpectedly, or do you know you're doing wrong as you do it? Can you give a few examples? If you ever find yourself becoming insensitive or calloused about the significance of your sin, read Isaiah 53 (which is a prophetic reference to Christ dying on the cross for your sins). Why does God need to go to such extremes in dealing with sin? In what ways does His perspective about sin differ from yours?

4. Eve made a big mistake by continuing to look at the forbidden fruit. Read Matthew 4:1-11; 1 Corinthians 10:13; and James 4:7. What strategies can you learn from these passages that will keep you from sinning? Christ resisted Satan's temptations, as you'll read in Luke 4:1-13. What do you find in Christ's responses that can help you resist Satan's schemes?

Chapter 5

Sin, now at full spread, must bring forth
death, and the first full-scale exercise of
judgment demonstrates that with God the
truth of a situation prevails, regardless of
majorities and minorities. If as "few" as
eight souls are saved, seven of these owe it
to a single one, and this minority inherits
the new earth. In a corrupt world Noah
emerges not merely as the best of a bad
generation, but as a remarkably
complete man of God.

—*Derek Kidner*

When It Rains, It Pours

The expression "when it rains, it pours" roughly stands for the proposition that when things are going bad, they often get worse. We aren't sure that expression has universal application, but it certainly seems to be an accurate description of the sinful conduct of human nature. Just when you think our predicament is as bad as it can get, it gets worse.

We aren't very far into the history of humanity at this point. Just a few generations. And already humanity's immorality is so bad that God decides to wipe the human population off the Earth and start over. But wait. One man evidences faith in God and reverence of Him. One man in the entire Earth's population. God will start over with him.

More Sin and the Downpour

Genesis 4–9

The further effects of Adam and Eve's sin are seen in the chapters that immediately follow the story of their sin in Genesis 3. If they didn't understand the concept of death when God said they would return to the dust, they got exposed to it with shocking reality in Genesis 4.

M Is for Murder

If you ever wondered about the effects of sin, think about this: Within the span of a few verses, sin destroys the tranquility of the Garden of Eden, and people begin killing each other. Two murders are reported in Genesis 4.

- Adam and Eve's son Cain murdered his brother Abel (4:1-16).

- Lamech, who breaks God's law by marrying two women, killed someone else in an act of apparent self-defense (4:19-24).

The frequency of violence and immorality continued to accelerate as the population increased. Mankind was getting worse instead of getting better.

Am I My Brother's Killer?

Adam and his family weren't totally cut off from God after the fiasco in the Garden. While they couldn't fellowship with God face-to-face as before, they could still pray to Him, worship Him, and present offerings of grain, other produce, or slain animals on an altar to Him.

Most everyone knows that Cain killed his brother Abel. But do you know what ticked Cain off? He was angry because God accepted Abel's animal sacrifice but not Cain's offering of fruits and veggies. This was not about God liking Abel more than Cain but about Cain's behavior.

Genesis 4:7 says that Cain did not respond to God in the right way. Some scholars suggest that God had given specific instruction to offer animal sacrifices. Other theologians say that offerings of produce were acceptable but that God rejected Cain's sacrifice because his inner attitudes were contrary to true worship.

One thing is clear. This was no accidental killing. Cain lured Abel into the field and then committed a cold-hearted, premeditated murder.

Murder in the Bloodline

A common theme throughout Genesis is that civilization doesn't get better; it gets worse. Even though the descendants of Adam and Eve were capable of making music and excelling at craftsmanship (4:19-22), they were tainted with the sin virus.

Lamech is an example of humanity's dark side. He was the world's first reported polygamist, and he killed a young man allegedly out of self-defense. But he seems both to brag about his status and justify the killing.

Are things any better today? Despite humanity's accomplishments, we are still suffering from the horrific effects of our sin.

Where Did All These People Come From?

When you read of Cain and Abel, you might think there were only four people on the Earth: Adam, Eve, and their two sons. So why was Cain afraid of retaliation by others for the murder of Abel (4:14)? "What others?" you may be asking.

Adam and Eve had lots of children. (They took God's command of 1:28 to "fill the earth" very seriously despite the pain of childbirth.) By the time Cain killed Abel, other adult children had started families. Remember that we don't know how old Cain was when he murdered Abel. But we do know that Adam was still producing children when he was 105 years old, and people back then lived to be 800 or 900 years old. (See Genesis 5.) God created Adam and Eve as adults, so they might have been only one or two years old when they started having kids. With a head start like that on their biological clocks, they could have produced a sizeable population by the time Cain was an adult.

If the scenario of marriage between the children of Adam and Eve sounds a little incestuous, don't let it bother you. Back then, marrying a sibling wasn't a problem. The human race was still genetically pure, so marrying a sibling produced no adverse side effects, and God didn't prohibit it.

He Is a Righteous Man, but Can He Float?

Genesis 6:5 sums up the extent and pervasiveness of evil in the world's population:

> *Now the LORD observed the extent of the people's wickedness, and he saw that all their thoughts were consistently and totally evil.*

Of all the people on Earth, only Noah worshiped God. Destruction of the rest of the world's population was a moral imperative for God. But God is patient and anxious for people to repent, so He gave Noah a building project that was so big nobody could miss it. And the construction took Noah so long (120 years) that everyone had ample opportunity to repent.

Don't be shocked that Noah took 120 years to build the ark and collect the animals. That was no ordinary boat he was building. We'll try to describe the dimension of the ark in terms you can visualize:

- It was as long as one and a half football fields.

- It was as high as a four-story building.

Experts estimate that as many as 45,000 animals could have fit into the boat.

A Man of Faith

Noah is not famous for his carpentry skills. And he is not renowned for his abilities as a sailor. He is known as a man of faith. Noah and his sons built the ark at a location that was probably miles from any large body of water. And at that time in history, a heavy mist watered the Earth instead of rain. No one in his or her right mind would have believed that the ark was ever going to float because no one had seen enough water to float it.

But sometimes God doesn't want us to make decisions based on what seems logical in a "right mind." Sometimes He asks us to respond in faith. And that's what Noah did:

> *It was by faith that Noah built an ark to save his family from the flood* (Hebrews 11:7).

How Big Was the Flood?

The story of the flood has captured the curiosity of people throughout history. And questions about the flood persist to this day. Is it a myth or a historical fact? Did the flood cover the entire Earth or just one region?

Some things are certain:

- The New Testament considers the flood to be an actual event.

- The occurrence of a single catastrophic flood is the most commonly repeated story in the traditions of ancient people.

- The ancient written historical accounts of the people from the Mesopotamian valley (where the

Bible places Noah) all include references to such a flood.

Some scholars, referred to as *universalists,* argue that the flood was a worldwide event. They believe that the flood affected the entire globe. They say the flood caused geological changes that triggered a thrusting of mountain ranges and a depression of sea beds.

On the other side of the argument are proponents of the "local flood" theory. They argue that a global flood would leave different evidence in the fossil record and in the rock strata. They believe the flood was limited to the region of the world's population at that time. After all, if God's purpose was to judge a civilization, a localized flood in the valleys of the Fertile Crescent would do the trick.

We aren't scholars, but we believe the following facts favor the universalist theory:

- Genesis 7:19-20 says that the tips of the tallest mountains were covered by the flood by at least 22 feet of water.

- The flood waters prevailed for five months, and Noah didn't disembark for seven more months. Noah and his family were shut up in the ark for 371 days. A flood that took a full year to subside must have been far-reaching.

- Genesis 7:11 refers to underground waters bursting forth in addition to the rain. That didn't happen on just one day. It continued for a long time, perhaps up to 150 days. (See 8:2.)

- An ark with deck space of 95,700 square feet was designed for a rather large flood.

- Noah and his family could have avoided a regional flood by moving to another part of the world. Traveling any distance would have been easier than spending 120 years building the ark.

Under the Rainbow

Almost immediately after reading that God created the world, you read that God almost destroyed all of it. In Genesis 9, with everyone back on ground, God lays down a few new ground rules. Some of these affirmative statements raise unanswered questions:

- Animal life was specifically permitted as food for human consumption (9:3). Does this mean that everyone before the flood was supposed to be a vegetarian?

- The death penalty was imposed for anyone who commits a murder (9:6-7). Does this mean God considers capital punishment to be an acceptable element in our system of justice, or was it necessary only for that time and culture?

- God identified the rainbow as a sign of His promise to never again destroy all life with a flood (9:8-17). Was the rainbow unknown until that time?

Theologians and scientists still ponder many questions concerning life on Earth before the flood. Some may never be answered in our lifetimes. But we can be sure of this: We live in a personal universe, and God, who created us, is a moral, righteous Being who has the power to judge and to save us.

■ ■ ■

$\mathcal{S}$tudy the $\mathcal{W}$ord

1. What wrong attitudes might Cain have had in his heart when his offering was rejected by God? (Check out Genesis 4:3-7; Hebrews 11:4; 1 John 2:9; 3:12.)

2. Read Matthew 24:37-39 and Luke 17:26-27 to see whether the New Testament considers the flood to be fact or fable.

3. Does 2 Peter 3:3-7 seem to indicate the flood was worldwide or just limited to a certain locality? Explain your answer.

4. Hebrews 11:7 describes Noah as a man of faith. According to this passage in Hebrews and what you read in Genesis, in what ways was Noah faithful? How was his faith challenged?

Chapter 6

Babel: 1. A city in Shinar in which Noah's descendants tried to build a very high tower to reach heaven and were prevented by God from doing so by a confusion of tongues; 2. an impracticable scheme

—*Webster's New World College Dictionary*

The High and Low of It

We are about to reach a highpoint of early humanity's self-centered achievement. But such occasions are often low points of human sin.

As you read this chapter, focus on humanity's attitude toward God. Think about their pride and sense of self-sufficiency. But don't be too critical of them because at the end of this chapter we'll be asking if you're harboring similar attitudes.

God Intervenes When Humans Scheme

Genesis 10–11

*Y*ou might be tempted to skip over chapter 10 of Genesis. It consists of three lists of the descendants of Noah's sons: Japheth (10:1-5), Ham (10:6-20), and Shem (10:21-32). We are the first to admit that reading names can be boring. Most of them are hard to pronounce, but occasionally you'll come across a few that will make you chuckle. (Our personal favorites in chapter 10 are Gomer and Nimrod.)

What's in a Name?

Before you formulate an opinion that reading the genealogies (lists of names in family bloodlines) is a waste of time, consider what the apostle Paul said:

> *All Scripture is inspired by God and is useful to teach us what is true and to make us realize what is wrong in our lives. It straightens us out and teaches us to do what is right* (2 Timothy 3:16).

That verse applies to Genesis 10, but we'll agree that the "useful" aspect is a little difficult to see at first glance.

Genesis 10 teaches us about the interrelationship of all peoples. This chapter gives a geographic list of the world's population at the end of the primeval age. The geography of these groups covers parts of Asia, Europe, and Africa. The populated region reached as far as the Iranian plateau in the east, the Mediterranean coastlands in the west, the Black Sea to the north, and south to what is now Somalia in Africa. Despite their geographic diversity, all of these people had something in common: their forefather, Noah.

Genesis 10 is important because it establishes the common ancestry of all people. No ethnic group is independent of another. No one segment of the population is superior to another. Since they all branched off of the same trunk of Noah's family tree, they are basically all the same.

This was not a popular concept among the people of the ancient Near East. Each tribe tended to believe that it was superior to others. As communities emerged, each locality developed its own cult and dedicated itself to the god of its cult. Many groups had a story in which their god founded them first and, of course, favored them above the rest of humanity.

But Genesis 10 shows that all nations and peoples came from God's blessings on the family of Noah. No one is disfavored in God's paradigm. Yes, God would later single out one group—the Jews—from the descendants of

Noah's son, Shem. But through the Jews, God planned to bring the blessing of Christ's salvation to all people. So in the upcoming chapters, when you see God getting involved with the Hebrews, He is not favoring some and excluding others; His plan for the Jews is intended for the benefit of all humanity.

Chapter 11 ends with more genealogies and the introduction of Abraham. He is the lead character in the next section, so we'll pick up his story in a few pages. For now, we'll focus our attention on a tower that is being constructed in the plains of Babylonia. You can't miss it. It is the only thing in the entire countryside that stands taller than a camel's hump.

The Tower of Power

The account of the Tower of Babel explains how the nations came to be scattered across the face of the Earth, all with different languages. Without this event, people across the globe would speak the same language (but the people in Texas would still speak with a drawl).

The Tower of Babel was the first significant building project mentioned in the Bible after the flood. The construction workers chose to make the tower out of fire-hardened mud instead of stone. This made sense because that region has lots of dirt but little stone. The tower was likely a prototype for the ziggurats that were prominent in early Mesopotamian settlements. Ziggurats look like the towers that toddlers make with their toy building blocks, with the blocks getting smaller as the stack gets higher. One such ziggurat in Babylon was 297 feet high. Most ziggurats were constructed as temples to pagan gods. The Tower of Babel might be further evidence that the generations after the flood wasted no time in returning to paganism.

When Genesis 11:5 says that "the LORD came down," it doesn't mean that He made a guest appearance in the city. There was no visible sign of His presence. Rather, it means that God intervened in the affairs and actions of the people.

Someone Call for an Interpreter

Giving the people different languages served two purposes. First, it showed the power of God (they obviously needed a reminder). Second, it served as a punishment.

God wasn't upset with the building project. He wasn't mad at the move toward urbanization. Cities and towers weren't the problem. Rebellion is what ticked off God. These people had wicked motives for their tower:

- They were resisting God's commandment to inhabit the whole Earth. (See Genesis 9:1.) Their expressed purpose was to avoid being "scattered all over the world."

- They wanted to provide a way to escape God's judgment if He sent another flood (which is why they wanted their tower to reach "to the skies").

- In their pride and arrogance, they considered themselves to be as great as God.

Remember that Moses was writing Genesis (and the other books of the Pentateuch) for the nation of Israel. This was his chance to give them some advice and guidance. He may have related the account of the Tower of Babel to remind them of the importance of obeying God. If they followed His precepts, then God would bless them.

But if they balked at His commands and acted in pride and rebellion, then God could scatter them. (Sure enough, Israel wasn't obedient to God, and over the course of the next several hundred years they were captured and scattered in exile.)

What Are Your Monuments?

The people who built the Tower of Babel wanted a monument to their own greatness. They wanted the attention and accolades instead of giving credit to God. We can easily be critical of them because their attempt to gain attention was so colossal. But we might be guilty of similar motives. Are you trying to take attention away from God? Do you think you are self-sufficient? Do you give God any credit for the accomplishments of your life? Make sure that you aren't building towers to your own greatness. God probably won't ever befuddle you with a foreign language, but He'll figure out an equally effective way to humble you.

Genesis Narrows Its Focus

As you read Genesis 11, get ready for a thematic megashift. It begins right after the story of the Tower of Babel as you embark into more genealogies. The first ten-and-a-half chapters of Genesis have a grand and global focus on God's dealings with the entire human race. But you were not reading mere stories that Moses told for historical significance; they were insightful lessons about the nature of humanity and the nature of God. So if you were paying attention, you already know some things about humanity and about God:

Human Nature Is Peculiar:

- God created men and women in His own image.

- We have the unique opportunity to have a relationship with God.

- But we have an innate bent toward evil.

God's Desire to Redeem Humanity Is Evident:

- He originally created humans to fellowship with Him.

- Adam and Eve fell and lost their home in the Garden, but God restored fellowship with humanity.

- Before long, humanity turned its back on God and plunged headlong into wickedness and immorality.

- So God imposed the judgment of the flood and got things back on track with righteous Noah and his family.

- But within a few generations, the inhabitants of the world were rebelling against God again, so God intervened with a judgment at Babel that separated them into various nations and regions.

And here is where the mega-shift begins. From this point forward, the rest of Genesis follows the story of a single family. Actually, the rest of the Old Testament focuses on that family (although it grew rather large over the succeeding generations). The patriarch of the family is Abraham. He was the one man God selected to start a new nation. God would use that man (Abraham) and that nation (Israel) to bring the message and plan of salvation to the world.

A Patriarch by Any Other Name Is the Same

Before he got famous, Abraham was just known as *Abram*. *Abram* wasn't a nickname, and it wasn't just a shorthand version for *Abraham*. His real name was *Abram*. God actually gave him the new name of *Abraham* in Genesis 17 (when God also changed the name of Abraham's wife from *Sarai* to *Sarah*). When we get to chapter 17, we'll tell you why God made the change. Until then, we'll stick with the original names.

The story of Abram gets rolling in Genesis 12, but Chapter 11 gives you some important background that you'll need to know:

- *Genesis 11:27-30.* Terah was a descendant of Shem (one of the sons of Noah). He lived in a city called Ur in a region of Mesopotamia (referred to as "Ur of the Chaldeans"). Terah had three sons including Abram. Abram married Sarai. She couldn't have kids.

- *Genesis 11:31-32.* Abram packed up his wife (Sarai), his father (Terah), and his nephew (Lot, who was the son of Abram's deceased brother). Together they headed off to the city of Haran (where Terah died at the ripe old age of 205).

And with that background, you are ready to jump into Genesis 12.

■ ■ ■

Study the Word

1. What does chapter 10 contribute to the story of Genesis?

2. Babylon appears throughout the Bible. Look at Isaiah 13:1–14:23; 47:1-5; Jeremiah 20:1-6; 25:1-14; 50–51; Revelation 18. How do these passages influence your opinion of the rebellious attitudes of the people building the Tower in Babylon?

3. The Tower of Babel wasn't the only place God used different languages. Read the story in Acts 2:6-11. Do you find any similarities in God's purposes for using various languages in Genesis 11 and Acts 2?

4. Make a list of the specific reasons that the people stated for building the tower. Now make a list of the effects of what happened to the people after God imposed His judgment. What does this tell you about the wisdom of disobeying God's commands?

The Beginning of God's Covenant

Chapter 7

It was by faith that Abraham obeyed when God called him to leave home and go to another land that God would give him as his inheritance. He went without knowing where he was going. And even when he reached the land God promised him, he lived there by faith—for he was like a foreigner, living in a tent…Abraham did this because he was confidently looking forward to a city with eternal foundations, a city designed and built by God.

—*Hebrews 11:8-10*

*A*bram

Abram is one of our heroes. We know he's not the usual kind of hero. He is not a popular Halloween costume character, and we doubt that any teenagers have a poster of him hanging on their bedroom wall. But he followed God in a way that both convicts and encourages us.

Abram wasn't perfect. Far from it. But that is one of the reasons we can relate to him. His failures give us hope that we are not totally disqualified from serving God when we mess up. But he is not one of our heroes because of his failures; his faith is what we admire. He had faith not only to believe in God but also to follow Him. Saying you believe is relatively easy, but stepping out in faith and following where God leads is much more difficult. Abram followed God in a big way. Most of us would have made up some excuse if we had been in similar circumstances. That's what makes Abram a hero. He followed God without questions or complaints.

If you haven't had the opportunity to meet Abram "up close and personal" before, now is your chance. We think you'll like him. You might even wish you had a poster of him to hang on your bedroom wall.

When God Called,
Abram Answered

Genesis 12

*Y*ou'll make a mistake if you view the next few chapters of Genesis as a biographical sketch of Abram. Yes, Abram is prominent, but he is not the main character. You'll really be reading about the God of Abram. Abram's character and conduct may provide you with a pattern for your own faith, but remember that God's grace and mercy provide the foundation and encouragement for our faith.

As you read the initial verses of Genesis 12, you will see that God called Abram while he was living in Haran. Actually, this may have been the second time that God called upon Abram to follow His direction. Acts 7:2-4 says that when the Terah clan was living in Ur, God appeared to Abram:

> God told him, *"Leave your native land and your rel-*
> *atives, and come to the land that I will show you"*
> (Acts 7:3).

This would mean that the first time God spoke to Abram, He called Abram out of his homeland of Ur. But how far did God lead Abram? We know the eventual final destination was Canaan, but was Haran an intentional stopping point? Some scholars think Abram showed a lack of commitment when he stopped in Haran (perhaps remaining there due to his father's declining health). Others think Abram was awaiting God's timing for further directions to the place (Canaan) that God had not yet revealed to Abram.

The Person of God's Call

Back in Genesis 3:15, God indicated that He was going to send a Savior to the world. Remember that dialogue with Satan in the Garden of Eden? Even if you have forgotten it, God didn't. He chose Abram to be the individual through whom He would fulfill that promise. Abram would be the father of the Jewish nation. From this one man, God was going to bless the entire world.

When Abram was in Haran, God reinitiated His call for Abram to pack up and hit the road, and Abram obeyed. Just as when he had left Ur, Abram had no idea where he was going.

God routed the caravan of Abram, Sarai, and Lot (along with their servants and flocks) to Canaan. This was the land that God had selected for Abram. It is the region that was later known to the Jews as "the Promised Land" because God had promised it to Abram.

Abram is known as a man of faith. He is a charter member of the "Hall of Fame of Faith" in Hebrews 11. He believed and followed God despite serious challenges:

- He did not know where he was going (Hebrews 11:8).

- He did not know how God's promises were going to be accomplished (Hebrews 11:11).

- He did not know why God asked him to do certain things (Hebrews 11:17-18).

If you think that Abram was some vagrant sheepherder, then you might think following God's call was no big deal for him. But it was a big deal because he wasn't a sheepherder and Ur was no hick town.

- Abram lived in Ur in about 2000 B.C. It was a well-developed city near the Persian Gulf and was a center for commerce in the region. Archaeologists report that middle-class homes in Ur at that time had 10 to 20 rooms with adequate provisions for servants and guests. Many of the homes were two stories high and had indoor plumbing. Tombs in that region dating back to 2500 B.C. contained magnificent jewels and musical instruments. The children in Ur were well-educated, and the society offered many cultural events and amenities.

- Abram's family enjoyed all that Ur had to offer. His family was successful in commerce (most likely with sheep and other livestock). He was in the upper echelon of society.

So when God called Abram to leave Ur and to go to some mystery spot, Abram had to make a decision. Would he stay in the luxury of Ur with the likelihood of a prosperous future and an easy life, or would he abandon his family and friends for a life of uncertainty?

The Promises of God's Call

The *where* of God's call was a secret, but the *why* wasn't. God's call to Abram included certain promises. Referred to as God's *covenant* with Abram, here is what God promised:

- God would make Abram the father of a great nation.

- God would bless Abram.

- God would make Abram a blessing to others.

- God would bless those who were kind to Abram and curse those who opposed him.

- God would use Abram to be a blessing to all of humanity.

We can figure out what all of this means because we can look at these promises with the help of the entire Bible and 4000 years of history (neither of which were available to Abram). We know that Abram's descendants, the Jews, were God's chosen people. In Old Testament times, these "Children of Israel" received God's blessings as He made Himself known to the world through them. Even more importantly, one of the descendants of Abram, Jesus Christ, is the Savior of the entire world. So we can easily understand the promises that were associated with

God's call. But without a doubt Abram was befuddled by it all. Nonetheless, he did what God asked.

The Paradox of God's Call

Both Ur and Haran were cities of paganism and immorality. (Does that surprise you?) Abram's friends and the family members he left behind in both cities must have scoffed at him for leaving. Can you blame them? From all appearances, the promises that God gave to Abram seemed unbelievable:

- God took him away from his homeland and promised him new land that wasn't identified.

- God promised to make him the patriarch of a great nation, but he and his wife were too old to be able to have children.

- When Abram finally arrived at God's destination of Canaan, hostile residents occupied it.

- God promised Abram all sorts of blessings, but he arrived in Canaan during a famine.

A Detour and Deception in Egypt

After a short time in Canaan, Abram made a temporary side trip to Egypt with his clan to escape a famine. Was this a spiritual default on his part? Some theologians say his faith faltered, and he should have stayed in Canaan and trusted God for his provision. Other theologians say God could have directed him to Egypt (but that conversation just isn't reported by Moses) or that God allowed Abram to use common sense and figure out a way to get food (like when you walk to the refrigerator without waiting for a sign from God when your stomach is growling).

Personally, we aren't critical of Abram for going to Egypt to put an end to his hunger pains. Remember that we're inclined to give him the benefit of the doubt because he is one of our heroes. But he had no excuse for what he did in Egypt.

Abram was afraid that people in Egypt would notice the beauty of Sarai. As word of her beauty spread throughout the country, Pharaoh would want her in the palace harem. This might mean that Pharaoh would kill Abram to get him out of the way.

Just in case this was going to happen, Abram devised a dishonest scheme. He told Sarai to lie and say she was his sister. Abram's plan wouldn't keep Sarai out of the harem, but it would keep him alive.

Things turned out exactly as Abram had suspected. (This means that Sarai really must have been a beauty because she was 65 years old at the time.) Pharaoh took Sarai into the harem and rewarded her "brother" Abram with lots of gifts (servants, flocks of sheep, and herds of cattle and camels). But God brought a plague on Pharaoh's household, and he finally figured out that God was judging him because Sarai was Abram's wife. Pharaoh kicked Abram and Sarai out of the country, but they were allowed to keep all that he had given to them. (Pharaoh might have been tempted to kill Abram, but he was probably afraid of a fate worse than plagues if he did so. He knew enough not to mess with Abram's God.)

Don't think that the story had a great ending. Abram had failed God. He had enough faith to trust God with his location, but not enough faith to trust God with his life. And the wealth he received on the trip proved troublesome. As you are about to read, those riches caused a rift between Abram and Lot, and one of the servant girls caused a problem in Abram's marriage.

Abram was applying the doctrine of situational ethics. He based his morality (deciding lying was a good idea) on circumstances. In other words, he lowered his standards to work himself out of a tough situation. But this is never God's way. Are you guilty of the same thing from time to time? Do you find yourself lying to get out of tough circumstances? Do you rationalize or justify behavior that offends God? No ends justify sinful means.

◼ ◼ ◼

$\mathcal{S}$tudy the $\mathcal{W}$ord

1. Abram had faith to believe in God. And his faith was strong enough to go where God led him. Read Hebrews 11:1 for a definition of faith. Now describe faith in your own words.

2. God's covenant with Abram isn't exactly clear in this passage. This early covenant contains the essence of God's plan to redeem humanity. When we get to Genesis 15–17, we'll cover it in more detail. For now, read Jeremiah 30–31 and Hebrews 7–10 to get a fuller picture of the covenant. Summarize that covenant as if you were God explaining it to Abram.

3. Reread the promises of Genesis 12:2-3,7. Notice that these are unconditional promises. What is the significance of that?

4. Imagine that you are Abram, and God calls you to leave Ur. What excuses might you (as Abram) give? Now imagine that God is calling you (the real you) to make some major change in your life's situation. Would you be willing to make a change? What would cause you to hesitate?

Chapter 8

The contrasting destinies of Abram and Lot provide additional evidence why Abram had to leave Haran and move about in order to serve Yahweh wholeheartedly. Living in a sparsely settled land outside the urban centers, Abram could worship Yahweh and at the same time gain a reputation as a noble sheik. Lot, by contrast, ended up in Sodom and sought to become a citizen of that wicked city. In order to be accepted by the citizenry, he had to place his principles at risk....Lot came to a tragic end. By contrast, Abram grew stronger and wealthier.

—*John E. Hartley*

He Didn't Play It Safe

Abram's faith in God was revealed not only by his cross-country trek from Ur and Haran to the land of Canaan but also in his daily actions.

In these next two chapters of Genesis, you'll see Abram risk everything from his wealth to his own life. Here is a man who had a lot to live for.

- He already had considerable wealth, but God had promised far more.

- He was still childless yet waiting for God to fulfill the promise of descendants.

Abram had much to lose, but amazingly, he was willing to risk it all—and all for the sake of his flaky, unappreciative nephew, Lot.

As you read this next section, consider if you trust God enough to put everything that you have at risk as you follow God's direction. Do you have that kind of faith in God's promises to provide for you?

A Lot of Trouble

Genesis 13–14

*U*p to this point, Lot (Abram's nephew) has been a minor player. Since his dad died at a young age (Genesis 11:27-28), Lot had become like an adopted son in Abram's family. He tagged along when Abram left Ur, and he continued with the family when they departed from Haran for the Promised Land. But he was nothing more than a bit player in the unfolding drama.

In these two chapters of Genesis, however, the spotlight moves to Lot. Actually, you might say he elbowed his way to center stage. In these two chapters, we see Lot in a starring role. But what we see is not a pretty picture.

Although the focus will be on Lot, don't forget to notice how God continues to work in the circumstances of Abram's life. Whenever events seem to go the wrong way, God turns things around. The fulfillment of the covenants was never in jeopardy although the situation may suggest otherwise. Abram was apparently confident in all of this because his faith is unwavering regardless of the circumstances.

A Choice with Consequences

When Abram and his tribe returned to the land of Canaan, trouble began with his upstart nephew, Lot. They played out the classic "this town isn't big enough for the both of us" routine. Abram could have pulled rank on Lot, but he didn't. Instead, he let Lot be the one to choose who would get which section of the country. The choice was between two regions:

- The Jordan Valley to the north was fertile farmland.

- The land of Canaan, where they were, was dry and desolate.

Lot was a fool (as you'll soon discover), and he was also selfish, so he didn't hesitate to pick the land to the north. After he made his choice, Lot packed up his family and his riches and moved to the hills just outside the wicked city of Sodom. This episode revealed the true nature of both men. Abram was gracious. Lot was selfish, worldly, and foolish.

This was no simple decision to be made arbitrarily by some sort of "rock-paper-scissors" method. The choice involved significant consequences:

- Abram dealt with Lot righteously, and God made sure Abram knew that God was honored by his decision. In 13:14-18 God reaffirms the earlier covenant to give the land to Abram and his descendants. So Abram hadn't lost anything by trusting in God's promises. In the long run, the land that Lot chose would eventually belong to Abram's descendants.

- Lot's consequences weren't so positive. In fact, they were disastrous as we soon find out. As you read the events that occur in Genesis 14, just remember that this was the land that Lot chose in what he thought was a shrewd move.

Abram to the Rescue

Lot quickly got into trouble. That's what happens when you get drawn into the worldly customs of a pagan society. The problems didn't happen all at once. At first he had lived outside of the city. But the immorality of Sodom was attractive to him, and before too long he had abandoned his tent in the country for a house in the city.

The same wealth that attracted Lot was also appealing to foreign invaders. Local residents had endured 13 years of fierce territorial battles. But the armies of Sodom and Gomorrah finally faltered in the defense of their cities. Invading forces plundered the city of Sodom and captured Lot as a hostage.

When Abram received the message that his nephew was in trouble, he immediately formed a posse of his own servants. After a trek of about 120 miles, Abram initiated a military attack in the middle of the night. He routed the enemy. In addition to rescuing Lot, Abram saved many other hostages. He collected all of the stolen booty and led the captives back to their homelands.

$\mathcal{M}$uch to $\mathcal{L}$ose

We get a picture of Abram's wealth when we read that he collected 318 men from his household servant staff to form the militia that rescued Lot. Each of these men may have been married with at least one child. That means that Abram's "household" was over 1000 people. Imagine the cost of the daily overhead to feed those people. Imagine the size of his herds and farmland to keep all of those people fully employed. Now imagine how much he had to lose in a battle that didn't concern himself personally.

True Rewards

As he returned home after rescuing Lot, Abram was greeted by two kings. The same invaders who captured Lot had terrorized their countries. Both kings wanted to honor Abram.

- Melchizedek, the king of Salem, was also a priest of the true God. He brought Abram an offering of bread and wine.

- The king of the pagan city of Sodom offered to let Abram keep all of the wealth that had been stolen from Sodom.

Abram was quick to reject the offer from the king of Sodom. He didn't want anything to do with that wicked city. He was equally quick to accept the offering of Melchizedek. In fact, to acknowledge that God had given him victory, Abram gave Melchizedek one-tenth of all of the wealth he recovered in the battle. In other words, Abram refused to align himself with the pagan city of

Sodom or in any way gain a financial advantage from its citizens. He took nothing for himself or his men. (If you are wondering whether God honored Abram's stance, you'll discover the answer in Genesis 15.)

*M*elchizedek

As we were writing this book, we were tempted to skip over the episode of Abram's rescue of Lot and his encounters with Melchizedek and the King of Sodom. After all, Genesis is full of battles, and we can't highlight all of them. But Melchizedek deserves mention, and not just because his name means "king of righteousness" or because he was the king of Salem (which means "peace").

Hebrews 7 makes an extended reference to Melchizedek. If the writer of Hebrews believed that Melchizedek deserved special attention, then we thought we ought to give it to him.

According to Hebrews 7, Melchizedek should be viewed as a type of Christ, whose priesthood ranked above that of Aaron. Hebrews seems to suggest that Melchizedek did not assert his priesthood because of lineal descent in a priestly family. Instead, God specifically appointed him to the priesthood. Thus, Melchizedek is a picture of Christ. Jesus did not become a priest because of His lineage. Instead, Christ is our High Priest because of God's divine selection.

■ ▦ ▦

Study the Word

1. What values motivated Lot to select the Jordan Valley and stick his uncle with the land of Canaan? What can you tell about Abram's values from his decision to give Lot the first choice? In what ways do your values affect your choices?

2. Lot's spiritual decline began when he left the influence of his godly uncle. The downward spiral continued when he moved near Sodom, and he hit bottom when be became a prominent citizen of that pagan city. How could Lot have prevented those stages of spiritual disintegration? What practical steps does Psalm 1:1-2 suggest?

3. Melchizedek is a representative type of Christ (who is our King and Priest). Read about him in Hebrews 5–7. The bread and wine (Genesis 14:18) were symbols for the body and blood of Christ. Just as Melchizedek greeted Abram with a meal after a battle, Christ provides us with help when we need it. Describe the ways in which Melchizedek foreshadows the person and work of Jesus Christ.

4. Abram gave Melchizedek a portion of his wealth. This was an act of worship, acknowledging God's priority in Abram's life. What does this suggest to you about how you should worship God with your finances?

Chapter 9

Believers have often found themselves in the gulf between divine promise and personal experience: God's promise is clear but circumstances do not seem to be leading to its fulfillment. The failure in these situations is not God's but man's. What is true of believers today was true of Abram. God had given him a great promise, but events raised such deep questions in his heart that he began to fear.... In Genesis 15–17 God resolved that dilemma.

—*John J. Davis*

All of a Sudden...Not So Sure

Have you ever taken a certain course in your life because you were convinced that God was directing you that way...only to be frustrated by the outcome? We know what you were thinking (because we've been there ourselves). All of a sudden, you weren't so sure that you heard God correctly in the first place. You didn't doubt God's control of the universe; you just wondered if some communication problem developed between you and God. Maybe you didn't get the right signals, and now you should take matters into your own hands to get your life back on track.

This is where we find Abram by Genesis 15. More than a decade has passed since God promised that Abram would have a child, and still nothing. Abram needed a little reassurance from God. So that's exactly what God gave him. Unfortunately, Abram wasn't convinced, and he did exactly what you or I would have done—he took matters into his own hands to help God along a little bit.

All About the Covenant

Genesis 15–17

*G*od had mentioned the covenant with Abram in Genesis 12:1-3. He expanded on it a bit in Genesis 13:14-18. Now, in chapters 15–17, God gives Abram the full, unabridged version. This is a time of testing for Abram (and for Sarai). As you'll see, waiting was difficult, and sometimes they didn't wait long enough.

The Panic and the Promise

When this story picks up, Abram is 85 years old. He has been living in Canaan for ten years. He had been a patient man, faithful to God. But he was starting to show signs of cracking under the stress. God had talked about making Abram the father of a great nation, but nothing seemed to be happening. Abram was starting to panic: He had no child. How could he be the father of a great nation if he didn't have any descendants?

By this time, Abram and Sarai were not likely to produce any children. They had been trying for a long time with no results. With Abram at age 85 and Sarai at age 75, their biological clocks had wound down to a few ticks and no tocks.

According to the customs and laws, if Abram died without an heir, all of his wealth would pass to his highest-ranking servant. In such cases, the otherwise childless couple adopted the servant. Could this be what God wanted?

All of the material possessions that Abram had were meaningless to him without what he really wanted—a child. In his culture, being childless brought great shame and humiliation (especially for Sarai). This was a crisis of faith for Abram and Sarai. It was something that weighed heavily on them every day.

This is the background and context for Genesis 15. God reassured Abram that everything was under control.

- God explained He would fulfill His promises through Abram's own bloodline. Abram didn't need to worry about adopting his servant.

- God showed Abram the evening sky and said his descendants would be more numerous than all the stars that Abram could see.

- God displayed the sacredness of the covenant with a firepot and a torch that passed miraculously through the middle of animals that Abram had prepared for a sacrifice.

Contracts and promises were serious business in the day of Abram. Two individuals making a contract would prepare a sacrifice of an animal. The carcass would be split into two pieces, and the two contracting parties would walk between the halves to seal the agreement. (It was messy, but at least they avoided using lawyers.) Abram didn't walk between the sacrificial animals. Only God went through, represented by the smoking firepot and the blazing torch. (Perhaps these are symbols of the cloud and the pillar of fire that led the Children of Israel through the wilderness for 40 years, as told in Exodus.) Abram didn't need to be part of the ceremony because this was a unilateral covenant. God was the only one making the promise.

The Mrs., the Maid, and the Master

Sarai didn't have the faith of her husband. She felt compelled to move things along if God wasn't going to fulfill His promise in the normal way. Perhaps partially in faith (knowing that God had promised Abram an heir), but certainly in desperation, Sarai schemed to use their maid, Hagar, as a sexual surrogate.

Sarai's plan worked. Hagar became pregnant. But the plan backfired. As you can imagine, tension grew between Sarai and Hagar. The animosity between the two women (and Sarai's jealousy) got so bad that Hagar fled.

Hagar was destitute and struggling alone in the desert. An angel of the Lord appeared to her and said she was pregnant with a son. The boy's name would be Ishmael (which means "God will hear"). The angel also said that the boy would grow up to be wild and rebellious. Hagar returned to Abram's family, but they eventually rejected Ishmael (see Genesis 21:8-21). Ishmael went on to have 12 sons of his own. His descendants are the Arab peoples, who have been enemies of the Jews for centuries.

Covenant Clarification

Another 13 years passed between the birth of Ishmael in Genesis 16 and the events of chapter 17. At this point, Abram was 99 years old and Sarai was 89. God was obviously waiting for a time when the birth of a child could be nothing other than a miracle.

To renew and reinforce the earlier covenant, God gave Abram and Sarai two reminders:

- *New Names.* Abram became *Abraham*. The name shift meant that the "high father" became "father of a multitude." And God changed Sarai's name too. No longer would she be known as *Sarai* ("the contentious one"); her new name was *Sarah* ("a princess").

- *A New Sign.* Circumcision was the mark that associated Abraham and his descendants with God and set them apart as God's chosen people.

---

*G*od in the *M*iddle

Bible scholar Matthew Henry has said that "ah" is the English abbreviation for Jehovah. He pointed out that "Abraham" is the result of putting "ah" in "Abram" (as in Abr-ah-am). That is literally what must have happened to Abram. He had God in the middle of his life. How else can you explain his continued devotion and faith in the promises of God when the circumstances appeared contrary? What about you? Are you living in a way that reflects God in the middle of your life?

■ ■ ■

Study the Word

1. Genesis 15 was particularly important to the apostle Paul. He built his case for our justification by faith on it. Read Romans 4 and Galatians 3. How does Genesis 15 apply to your salvation by faith in Jesus Christ?

2. Abram's choice of Sarai's maid to give birth to an heir was legally and socially acceptable. But what is legally and socially acceptable isn't necessarily within God's will. What attitudes toward God are revealed by their attempt? Can you think of an analogous situation in your life when you tried to help God move things along? What were your attitudes toward God?

3. Since the time of Christ, circumcision is no longer required for those who believe in God. Compare Genesis 15:6 and 17:1 with Galatians 5:6. Also see Romans 2:25-29. Instead of circumcision, what is required of today's Christians? Circumcision symbolized identity with the people of God. What are the signs of your identity with God's people?

4. Abraham was fretting about the circumstances of his life. God gave him some clear-cut reassurances. What circumstances do you worry about? Can you find reassurances from God in His Word? Review the covenants given in Genesis 15:9-21 and 17:2-14. What did God promise to do? What was Abram's only responsibility in the Genesis 15 passage? What did 17:9-14 add to Abram's responsibilities? What is the significance of this additional responsibility given to Abram?

Chapter 10

Lot may have been spared because of Abraham's intercession. Very often, no doubt, we enjoy the blessing of God because others have prayed for us. Folks may scoff at relatives who are servants of Christ, but they find it no disadvantage to have such relatives. Who knows how many a wandering son has been withheld from ruin because of a godly mother's prayers, or how often one Christian in a family delivers all from judgment? Sometimes the Lord blesses an undeserving husband so that a wife who is faithful to her Lord may be spared, and vice versa. If you are a child of God through faith in Christ, are you aware of your opportunities to bless, through your prayers, those you love?

—*Henry Jacobsen*

What Kind of God Would Do a Thing like That?

God is love. That is completely and utterly true. And the love of God is what most people like to focus on. But God is bigger than our concept of love. Yes, love is one of His characteristics and attributes, but it is only a part of who He is.

God has other attributes and characteristics. He is also holy and righteous. He is a God of judgment. He cannot tolerate sin. We must not ignore or forget these other personality traits of God.

And that is why this next passage of Genesis is so important.

A Divine Encounter, an Angelic Attack, and an Old Sin

Genesis 18–20

These three chapters describe three separate visits:

- Genesis 18: God visits with Abraham and Sarah

- Genesis 19: Angels visit Lot in the city of Sodom

- Genesis 20: Abraham and Sarah visit King Abimelech

Each one introduces significant spiritual lessons.

No Laughing Matter

The Lord Jesus Christ and two angels appeared to Abraham. Of course, Abraham didn't recognize Christ at first. He just thought they were strangers because they appeared in human form as ordinary travelers. But Abraham was a friendly guy, and he was anxious to show these travelers some hospitality.

Abraham soon learned that these were no ordinary hikers. Christ told Abraham that within a year's time Sarah would give birth to a son. Sarah, who was eavesdropping behind the tent flap, couldn't restrain her laughter. But she became sober when Christ asked her, "Is anything too hard for the LORD?" (18:14).

The angels left for an assignment in the cities of Sodom and Gomorrah, but Christ stayed behind to talk more with Abraham. He told Abraham about God's plans to destroy the cities of Sodom and Gomorrah for their wickedness. Abraham's nephew, Lot, lived in Sodom with his wife and daughters. Abraham pleaded for God to spare Sodom's destruction for the sake of Lot. God agreed to spare the city if even only ten God-fearing people lived there. Abraham knew that Lot had a wife, four daughters and two sons-in-law. That made eight. Abraham must have figured that Lot's family could have influenced at least two other people to believe in God. Abraham figured wrong.

Talking with Christ

Don't miss the significance of Abraham's encounter with Christ. Their friendship was rich. Christ felt comfortable and at home with Abraham. Perhaps that is why Abraham is known as "the friend of God" (James 2:23). Abraham's relationship with God is the type that Paul mentions in Ephesians 3:17 when he says, "I pray that Christ will be more and more at home in your hearts." Do you have that kind of relationship with Christ?

Take It with a Grain of Salt

The two angels went to visit Lot in Sodom. They gave Lot a chance to escape by warning him of God's plan to destroy the cities of Sodom and Gomorrah. Lot immediately told his married daughters and sons-in-law, but they thought he was joking. He had apparently never been serious about spiritual matters before. To think that he was serious now was a joke.

The angels didn't find ten God-fearing people in Sodom, so judgment came. Lot escaped with only his wife and his two single daughters. His wife was so enraptured by the culture that she couldn't resist looking back at it as she departed. This was in direct disobedience to the instructions they had received, and God immediately turned her into a pillar of salt.

The story of Lot ends tragically. We leave him as a cave-dweller where he commits incest with his daughters in a drunken stupor. We wonder if he ever regretted the choice he made when he and his uncle were picking places to live back in Genesis 13.

The lesson of Lot is one for all of us. We can get so caught up in the culture that it dilutes God's influence on us. What a contrast between Abraham and Lot. Abraham enjoyed God's blessings; Lot witnessed God's judgment.

The Same Old Sin

When you read Genesis 20, you might think it seems familiar. You're correct because this story and the story in the last half of Genesis 12 bear a striking and saddening similarity. Abraham is once again lying about his marriage when he enters a foreign land. Like before,

Abraham tells King Abimelech that Sarah is his sister. Again God intervenes and reveals the truth.

In Genesis 20:12, we learn that what Abraham said was partially true. Sarah was Abraham's half sister. They were both the children of Terah, but they had different mothers. But this wasn't an acceptable loophole to excuse what Abraham said to Abimelech, and Abraham knew it.

How could Abraham repeat the same sin? Apparently he hadn't judged it in his own life. He had confessed his sin after the Egypt episode (see Genesis 13:1-4), and it had been forgiven, but confessing sin is not the same as judging sin. When we judge our sin in our own life, we begin to see it the way God sees it. God hates our sin, and we will only put certain sinful conduct out of our lives when we have that same attitude toward it.

■ ■ ■

$\mathcal{S}$tudy the $\mathcal{W}$ord

1. The Lord rebuked Sarah's laughter but not Abraham's. What must have been the difference in the attitudes behind their laughter? What in Genesis 18:1-15 do you find relevant to your life?

2. Genesis 18:19 is a great summary of God's intent for His relationship with Abraham. Describe the characteristics of that relationship. Are similar characteristics present in your relationship with God? If not, why not? The strength of his relationship with God gave Abraham the courage to intercede on behalf of Lot. Who are the people that you are (or should be) praying for?

3. What have you learned about God in the ways that he dealt with Abraham, Sodom, and Lot? What do these things tell you about God's requirements of His people? What needs to change in your life to align yourself with what God requires?

4. You have read several instances in which Abraham or Sarah applied situational ethics to excuse sinful conduct. They thought they had to work their own way out of a touchy situation instead of leaving the situation to God. What principle can you learn from 2 Corinthians 12:9 that is applicable to such situations?

The Beginning of God's Chosen People

*C*hapter 11

The thread that runs throughout all fifty chapters of Genesis is that there is a secret to living and that we will never experience completeness of life until we have learned and experienced this secret. The secret is simple—yet so many people in this world tragically miss it. The secret is friendship with God. The secret of life is a personal, daily relationship with the living God who was in the beginning, who made the heavens and the earth, who created the human race in His own image, and who wants to have fellowship and a living relationship with the people He has so lovingly created.

— *Ray C. Stedman*

Abraham's Legacy

Bruce is an estate planning and probate lawyer, so he is interested in gifts and stiffs. Bruce's law specialty actually facilitates our friendship because we never fight over the hotel newspaper if we are traveling together. Stan reads the headlines and the sports page while Bruce is content to read the obituaries. As Bruce will tell you, those little news articles in the "obits" can tell you a lot about the legacy that someone leaves behind.

From this point to the end of Genesis, you'll be reading a type of obituary. The stories reveal the legacy that Abraham left to his heirs. They tell of his descendants and trace the family tree through several generations. These are the generations that formed the basis of the great nation that God promised to Abraham.

Don't think that you'll be stuck reading some boring stories of old dead people. Unlike the newspaper obituaries that are fascinating only to Bruce, these are stories of adventure and intrigue. If newspaper obituaries had all of the adventure of Genesis 21–50, even Stan would be reading them. Of course, then we would be fighting over the hotel newspaper.

Isaac: The Family Begins and Nearly Ends

Genesis 21–24

What's Ahead

- ☐ A Son Arrives...Finally
- ☐ An Ultimate Test of Faith
- ☐ Picking a Bride

*W*hen you read through chapters 12–20 of Genesis, you probably never doubted that God would fulfill His promises to Abraham. But you had an unfair advantage because you probably already knew how the story was going to end. Abraham and Sarah weren't so fortunate. Imagine how closely they watched the calendar from the day that Christ visited them and prophesied that Sarah would have a son within one year. But they didn't have to watch the calendar for long. Within three months, Sarah was pregnant. The birth of their son, Isaac, marked the beginning of the fulfillment of God's covenant to Abraham.

The rest of Genesis, from chapter 21 to the end, follows the adventures of the three generations that followed Abraham. Actually, his family didn't multiply very fast. Abraham and Sarah only had one son. Isaac must have liked small families because he only had two sons: Jacob and Esau. But Jacob picked up the pace of progeny production by having 12 sons. But wait—we are getting way ahead of ourselves. Let's go back and get Isaac out of the womb.

A Son Arrives...Finally

God always keeps His promises, but the fulfillment doesn't always happen within the time frame that we prefer (or expect). When God first told Abraham that he would be the father of a great nation, Abraham probably suspected that he would have a child before he was 100 years old and Sarah was 90. But their son wasn't born until they had reached those ages. This wasn't an unplanned pregnancy. Isaac's birth was part of God's plan from the beginning of the world.

By the time Isaac was two years old, he may have already sensed the tension with Hagar and Ishmael. Abraham loved Ishmael, but he followed God's instructions to send them on their way. God protected Hagar, and no harm came to her or Ishmael.

Ishmael and Isaac demonstrate God's plan of salvation. Ishmael was a child of the flesh (Sarah's attempt to work things out on her own); Isaac was a child of God's promise and His power. The flesh and the Spirit are in a constant struggle. Our salvation doesn't make the flesh go away. We still struggle with our old sin nature. But just as Abraham had to get Ishmael out of his household, we need to rid our lives of that old nature. If we don't, we'll continue to have tension and strife in our lives. (See Romans 13:14.)

An Ultimate Test of Faith

Sometimes God seems to test you in proportion to your faith. At least that's what He did to Abraham. Although Abraham had already proven himself to be faithful, God devised one final test of faith. He told Abraham to offer Isaac as a sacrifice.

- *A Shocking Request.* God's directions were clear. He instructed Abraham to offer Isaac as a burnt sacrifice. Notice that Abraham didn't question God's command.

- *An Immediate Response.* Abraham didn't stall either. The next morning, he packed up his son and the gear and began the three-day, 60-mile trek to an altar at Mt. Moriah. Although he had no idea what was happening, Isaac carried the wood for the fire.

- *Divine Restraint.* Isaac knew enough about sacrifices to know that they needed a sacrificial animal. When he asked about the sacrifice, Abraham simply said, "God will provide a lamb, my son." But Abraham was not expecting God to make a last-minute change of plans. He had Isaac on the altar and was ready to plunge the knife when God called a halt to everything.

- *The Covenant Reaffirmed.* In response to Abraham's great act of faithfulness, God again reaffirmed the covenant promises about the size and significance of Abraham's descendants.

Comparisons Worth Noting

The scene of Isaac on the altar is an Old Testament picture of Christ's sacrifice for us. Look at the similarities between Isaac and Christ:

- A lot of anticipation surrounded their births. Just as Abraham and Sarah were awaiting Isaac's birth, generations of Jews were awaiting the birth of the Messiah.

- God specifically promised their births and prophesied about them.

- The birth of each was a miracle.

- Mt. Moriah is in Jerusalem (2 Chronicles 3:1), the city where Christ was crucified.

- Isaac carried the wood for his sacrifice to Mt. Moriah; Christ carried the cross to Calvary.

- Isaac laid on the altar without protest. Christ went willingly to the cross.

And don't overlook this significant fact: God provided a ram for Abraham to sacrifice in the place of Isaac. Christ was the sacrifice that died in your place.

How Could God Ask Such a Thing?

Perhaps God wanted to see if Abraham loved God more than he loved Isaac. Of course, God knew in advance how Abraham would respond, so maybe the lesson was for Abraham. Abraham might have put his faith in Isaac as his sole descendant to accomplish God's promises. If that is so, then this event reminded Abraham that he needed to put his trust in God. And that's what Abraham did.

Picking a Bride

Archaeologists say that during Abraham's time period, parents commonly made long-distance arrangements back in their homeland for brides for their sons. But Abraham didn't make any such arrangements. He just sent his servant and trusted God with the selection process.

Abraham had been willing to put his son's life on the altar, so he was also willing to let God guide the selection of his son's bride. Abraham didn't want his son's wife to come from the pagan nations in Canaan, so he sent his servant back to Haran to find a suitable bride for Isaac. Was Abraham's expectation that God could direct the servant reasonable? Of course. This was the same Abraham that let God lead him out of Ur to a destination that was unknown to Abraham.

The servant found just the right woman: Rebekah. She lived in the village where Abraham's brother, Nabor, had settled. Rebekah was Isaac's second cousin.

■ ■ ■

$\mathcal{S}$tudy the $\mathcal{W}$ord

1. Abraham's obedience was evidence of his faith. He proved what he professed. Read James 2:14-26 and explain the relationship between faith and actions.

2. What does Hebrews 11:17-19 tell you about Abraham's faith when he put Isaac on the altar?

3. Use your knowledge of the relationship and contrasts between Hagar (and her son, Ishmael) and Sarah (and her son, Isaac) to explain Galatians 4:21-31.

4. Read 1 Corinthians 10:11, which says that the events in the Old Testament happened to those people as examples. What truths about God and your relationship with Him are exemplified in the story of God's choosing a bride for Isaac?

Chapter 12

Often the question is asked why God would bless such a scoundrel as Jacob, seeming even to reward his evil ways. By way of answer, it should be remembered that God calls followers not because of what they are but for what they may become by His grace. No one deserves the blessings of God. Second, God had made an unconditional covenant with Abraham and confirmed it to Isaac; that involved working through the natural descendants of Isaac, that is Jacob. Third, however dimly, Jacob apparently had some appreciation of the spiritual blessings of God's covenant.

—Howard F. Vos

The Message Behind the Stories

As you enter this next section (Genesis 25–36), you'll read of Abraham's death, read little bit more about Isaac, and then move on to the adventures of Jacob. But don't forget that something much bigger is going on here. Yes, these are interesting stories, especially if you are a student of human nature. The best and (more often) the worst of human nature is revealed by these guys. But the real story is about God working in the circumstances of their lives to fulfill His covenant with Abraham. Regardless of where the story line takes you, remember to place it within the context of the Abrahamic covenant. Sometimes you think that God has gone off course. But as with His dealings in your life, He always knows what He is doing even though His strategy is not obvious at first glance.

Jacob: A Life of Struggles

Genesis 25–36

*S*arah died when she was 127 and Abraham was 137. He lived for another 38 years, and during that time he married a woman named Keturah. She gave him six sons, and these descendants became known as the Midianites. Abraham died at the age of 175. He left Isaac as the beginning of the line of the Jews.

The Family Tree Branches Out

Genesis doesn't give us much information about Isaac. He was the son of a famous father, and he was the father of a famous son. So he gets passed over a bit. That's what makes the episode with Abimelech in Genesis 26 so interesting. Although most of Isaac's life is ignored, Moses took the time to tell the story of Isaac lying about Rebekah, saying she was his sister. Does that remind you of anyone? Abraham would have done Isaac a huge favor if he had been honest about his own sin so Isaac could have learned a lesson the easy way rather than the hard way. What does this teach you about parents' responsibility to build spiritual principles into the lives of their children?

Rebekah had difficulty getting pregnant. Isaac was a child of God's promise, and he knew that the covenant would only be fulfilled if he had children. God answered his fervent prayers, and Rebekah became pregnant with twins. She did not have an easy pregnancy, and God revealed that just as the twins were struggling against each other in the womb, they would fight with each other during life. In fact, they and their descendants would be bitter rivals. God also clearly stated that the younger son would prevail over the older son.

Abraham was 160 years old when Rebekah gave birth to his grandsons, Esau and Jacob. He must have been encouraged that Isaac was producing children, but this was still a far cry from God's promise to give him descendants that would be as numerous as the dust of the Earth (Genesis 13:16).

The two sons were born when Isaac was 60 years old. The firstborn was Esau. The second born was Jacob. In the culture and tradition of the times, the firstborn male was the heir to father's wealth, power, and prestige. But God knew that Jacob was better suited for the role of preserving the covenant, so God chose Jacob as the son who would receive the birthright from Isaac.

The Name Says It All

The first twin born was named *Esau* (which means "hairy"—and that's exactly what he was). The second twin came out of the womb grasping his older twin's heel, so he was named *Jacob* (which means "heel-gripper" or "supplanter"). Jacob's action at birth characterized what he would be doing for the next several decades as he tried to grab his brother's birthright.

As you read about the life of Jacob, you may wonder if God made a mistake. Why would God want the line of the Jews to go through Jacob? He seems like such a sleazy guy. Without a doubt, Jacob was a rascal. He was known as "the deceiver." But he didn't stay that way. Watch for the transformation in him as he matures. He finally learns to rely on God instead of his own schemes. Isn't that a good picture for all of us? We can try to manipulate the circumstances of our life for so long, but eventually we realize that we'll be better off letting God be in charge.

The Battle over the Birthright

As young men, the twins had already made a deal for the birthright. Esau sold it to Jacob for a bowl of stew. We don't think it was gourmet stew; Esau was just really hungry and let the cravings of his stomach override the functioning of his brain. But the sons had not settled the matter of the official blessing from their father, Isaac. And here we see the intrigue:

- Esau was the firstborn, so the birthright was rightfully his. But he had sold it in a weak moment. He thought the stew deal should be ignored. Jacob believed that a deal was a deal and didn't want any beef about it.

- Isaac favored Esau. He was going to give his blessing to Esau no matter what the two boys had decided.

- Rebekah favored Jacob. She was going to do whatever was necessary to make sure he got his father's blessing.

Jacob and Rebekah conspired to trick the aged and blind Isaac into blessing Jacob instead of Esau. Through fraud and deception, Jacob became the heir and the one through whom the covenant line would progress. Isaac could have rescinded the official blessing, but he reluctantly confirmed it instead.

As you can imagine, Esau was ticked off with all of Jacob's schemes. Always following his emotions instead of his brain, Esau vowed to kill Jacob. But Rebekah found out about Esau's plans and sent Jacob to her hometown of Haran to live with his uncle Laban. Jacob planned to stay with Laban until Esau simmered down.

A Labor of Love

Jacob stayed in Haran (northwest Mesopotamia) with Uncle Laban for 20 years. But his visit wasn't extended because of Esau's prolonged temper. Jacob fell in love with Laban's daughter, Rachel. Laban permitted the marriage of Jacob to Rachel, but he stipulated that Jacob work for him for seven years. Fair enough. But Laban was as devious with Jacob as Jacob had been with Isaac. Laban continually changed the work requirement, and he even switched brides on Jacob. When Jacob woke up in the morning after his wedding night, he discovered that he had married the older (less attractive) sister, Leah. The Bible contains no verse that reads, "What goes around, comes around," but this would be the place for one.

The deception in this family didn't subside. Jacob also married Rachel, and Rachel and Leah competed with each other to produce children. They even resorted to Sarah's old trick of getting credit for extra children by using their servants as sexual surrogates. And Laban was up to his old tricks of pulling a few switcheroos on Jacob. This forced Jacob to retaliate. The deception escalated until Laban's sons prepared to get involved because they believed they were being cheated. This was a good time for Jacob to make a break. At God's direction, Jacob packed up his wives and his children and his flocks and cattle (the ones that he had rightfully earned), and he headed back home to Canaan.

Going Back Home

An old adage says, "You can never go home again." Like most adages, we aren't sure what it means. But we know it isn't true when God tells you to go home. That's what He did with Jacob.

Jacob had grown rich and prosperous in Haran (despite Laban's continual ploys to cheat him). Jacob had also matured and begun to rely upon the Lord. And in Genesis 31:3, God told Jacob to return to Canaan, the land of his father Isaac.

In some respects, returning to Canaan could have been a no-brainer for Jacob:

- Canaan was the Promised Land for the descendants of Abraham. Jacob was the one through whom the covenant would be fulfilled, so his return to Canaan only made sense.

- Laban was getting more disenchanted with Jacob as time went on. Maybe Laban realized that Jacob wasn't as naïve as Laban thought.

- Laban's sons resented Jacob's success, and they started to plot against him.

Under such circumstances, the decision to leave Canaan seems obvious. But wait! Consider a few important things:

- Jacob was doing all of the work that made Laban rich. Laban was not going to let his meal ticket walk out of town.

- The sons of Laban had their eyes on Jacob's wealth. They wouldn't let him leave until they had successfully stolen from him.

- Esau was waiting back in Edom (the neighboring region of Canaan). An older brother never forgets when he has been swindled by his younger brother. Nothing is worse than an older brother with a good memory, an explosive temper, and his own private army.

Staying in Haran was Jacob's easiest option. But he followed God's directive and planned his escape. He snuck away in the middle of the night—no easy feat because he had his wives, his children, his servants, and his flocks to take with him. (If you are trying to get a mental picture, imagine the Ringling Brothers Circus, Disney On Ice, and the Garth Brooks Farewell Tour trying to sneak in and out of your town without being noticed.)

We see Jacob's maturity and especially God's protection and provision in the events of Jacob's sojourn to Canaan.

Jacob made peace with Laban. Laban chased down Jacob, but the two made a peace pact.

Jacob made peace with Esau. Jacob wasn't sure how Esau would respond. Esau and his gang were likely to attack Jacob's clan as soon as they saw the caravan on the horizon. Jacob used a strategy that was customary in the Middle East at that time. He divided his group into two sections and sent them on different paths. If Esau attacked one section, the other might be able to escape. Fortunately Jacob softened the heart of his brother with a peace offering of flocks and herds.

Have You Ever Wrestled with God?

Before he entered the Promised Land, Jacob said a prayer of dedication. It provides us with a pattern that we can use when we embark to follow God's directions (Genesis 32:9-12):

1. Jacob repeated the command that he had received from God. He put himself into the context of God's covenant to Abraham. We can do the same thing when we realize our place in God's will.

2. Next he acknowledged his unworthiness. This was a huge step in Jacob's maturity. Before, he would have relied on his own wits and powers of deception, but now he was recognizing that he was completely dependent upon God.

3. Then in humility he asked for God's protection and provision.

4. Finally he reminded himself of God's promises.

But apparently a few unresolved spiritual issues remained in his life. On the night before he entered the Promised Land, he couldn't get to sleep. As he lay awake, an angel of the Lord confronted him (some scholars say that it was the preincarnate Christ). They engaged in a power struggle. In the end, Jacob relinquished. The episode was symbolic of Jacob's entire life. He had tried to do things his own way, but the blessing of the Promised Land would be his only if he surrendered his will to God's will.

And if we learn that lesson from Jacob, we won't find ourselves wrestling with God. We will save ourselves a lot of grief in the long run.

"The Children of Jacob" Just Doesn't Have a Ring to It

What does the phrase "the Children of Israel" bring to your mind? Are you thinking about the land of Israel situated on the eastern edge of the Mediterranean Sea? Or are you thinking about the nationality of Israelites? You should be thinking about Jacob. During the wrestling match, at Genesis 32:28, God renamed Jacob as *Israel*. Because the Jews trace their ancestry through Jacob (Israel), they are often referred to as *the Children of Israel*. The 12 sons of Jacob became the forefathers of the respective 12 tribes of Israel.

■ ■ ■

$\mathcal{S}$tudy the $\mathcal{W}$ord

1. Abraham trusted God to pick out a bride for Isaac
    (Genesis 24). But the next generation was scheming
    over the birthright, and God never entered their con-
    siderations. How do these approaches influence your
    opinion of how decisions should be made?

2. Read Hebrews 12:16 to see why God may have pre-
    ferred to fulfill the convenant through the lineage of
    Jacob rather than Esau. What other traits marred
    Esau's character?   *godless*

3. Do you think Jacob's deception towards Isaac had
    anything to do with the deception Laban pulled on
    Jacob?

4. What does God's wrestling with Jacob tell you about God's desire to deal personally with His children? Is God wrestling with you over any issues or circumstances in your life?

Chapter 13

The Joseph story, though different in style
from that of the patriarchs, continues the
theme of the patriarchal narratives—God
overcomes obstacles to the fulfillment of the
promise....Joseph himself gives us a
theological grid through which to view the
events of his life....God reveals himself in
the life and the story of Joseph to be a God
in control of even the details of history.
From a human perspective, it appears that
Joseph falls prey to ill luck.... Joseph,
however, is aware that God is the one
behind the events of his life....This theme,
that God overrules the wicked intentions of
men and women in order to save his people,
runs throughout the Old Testament, but
perhaps nowhere more explicitly than
in the Joseph narrative.

—*Raymond B. Dillard and
Tremper Longman III*

The Good, the Bad, and the Ugly

If you invented your own religion, you'd probably tell glowing stories of the heroism of the patriarchs of your phony faith. After all, you'd want to attract followers by impressing them with the admirable qualities of the founders of your religion.

But Moses revealed the deep, dark, shameful secrets of Abraham, Isaac, and Jacob. Sure, they did a few things right from time to time. But these men were not paragons of virtue. They often made huge mistakes. So what was Moses thinking by giving a supermarket tabloid exposé of the patriarchs?

Remember that Moses wasn't promoting a religion based on the credibility of humans. Genesis isn't the story of a religion invented by mankind. It's all about God and the relationship He desires to establish with us. Aren't you glad that God is accustomed to working with imperfect humans? If God can use the likes of Abraham, Isaac, and Jacob, He can use you (and even us!), warts and all. He isn't looking for perfection, just obedience.

In contrast to some of his ancestors, Joseph seems to be consistent in his virtue and his acceptance of God's direction in his life. Character of that sort in anyone is admirable. But when you see the challenges that God allowed to occur on Joseph's life journey, you'll be particularly amazed. Maybe Joseph knew what we need to realize: God is large and in charge.

Joseph: It Was No Mere Coincidence

Genesis 37–50

*P*op quiz time! Name the promises that were part of the covenant that God made to Abraham. We'll get you started: God promised that He would [insert your answer here]. Okay, it's time to check your answers. This is a self-graded exam, so you are on the honor system. The correct responses would include reasonable facsimiles of these:

- God would make Abraham the father of a great nation with descendants more numerous than the grains of sand in the ocean.

- God would bless Abraham and his descendants.

- God would give Abraham and his descendants a promised land.

- God would bless the world through Abraham (the Savior of the world would come through his descendants).

Notice how much of the covenant is wrapped up in the *descendants* of Abraham. Jacob is only two generations from Abraham; Jacob's sons get us to three generations. We aren't very far out on a branch of the family tree. What a terrible time for a famine to hit Canaan and threaten to kill Jacob and all of his family! But wait! What if God sends them down to Egypt for the duration of the famine? Nah, that won't work. The Egyptians probably wouldn't extend any hospitality to the Canaanite inter-lopers. And besides, the famine is going to hit Egypt as well, so the Egyptians won't have any food to spare. Unless...

Don't be misled. You might think that the rest of Genesis is all about Joseph. He is mentioned a lot, but the real story is about how God is doing advance planning to protect and preserve the descendants of Abraham. You see, when God makes a promise, He takes care of all the necessary details to make sure that things happen just as He said they would.

He Had Everything but Tact

Abraham had one son: Isaac. Isaac had two sons: Esau and Jacob. Jacob decided to pick up the pace, so he had 12 sons. The acceleration was made easier because he involved two wives and two maidservants in the process.

However, they did not share an equal distribution of labor (pun intended). You'll find the names of the sons (and their mothers) listed in Genesis 35:23-26:

- Wife Leah gave birth to six sons.

- Leah's maidservant, Zilpah, gave Jacob two sons.

- Wife Rachel had two sons.

- Rachel's maidservant, Bilhah, added two more sons.

Of all the women in his life, Jacob loved Rachel the most. None of the others even came in a close second. So no one was surprised that Jacob's favorite was Joseph (Rachel's firstborn son). Jacob didn't keep his favoritism a secret, and he lavished attention and gifts on Joseph, including a fancy robe of fine linen. Joseph welcomed this preferential treatment, but Joseph's ten older brothers didn't tolerate it very well.

The gift of the ornamental robe (a status symbol) to Joseph designated him as Jacob's principal heir and successor. This wouldn't have upset younger brother Benjamin, but it enraged each of Joseph's ten older brothers, who believed they had a superior claim to heirship than Joseph.

The friction between Joseph and his older brothers intensified because Joseph didn't display much tact when he told the family about his vivid dreams.

- In one dream, everyone was busy binding sheaves of grain. The sheaves seemed to come alive. Joseph's sheaf of grain stood tall, and all of the sheaves of the other family members bowed down to his.

- In another dream, the sun and moon and 11 stars were bowing down to Joseph. The brothers didn't need to make a call to the psychic hotline to figure out that the sun and moon represented their parents, and they were the 11 other stars.

Jacob's sons already had plenty of sibling rivalry, but Joseph's blabbing about his midnight visions was making him Public Enemy Number One with his brothers. So they did what all brothers do when they have a grudge against a younger brother: They sold him into slavery.

And You Thought the Strongest Man Who Ever Lived Was Samson

Remember our hint that the rescue of Jacob's family from the famine would occur in Egypt? Well, just where do you think those slave traders who purchased Joseph were headed? That they were traveling to Egypt was no mere coincidence.

Joseph was 17 or slightly older when his brothers sold him into slavery. By the age of about 23, he had worked himself into a position has chief servant for the household of Potiphar. As a high-ranking official in Pharaoh's administration, Potiphar had all the luxuries and benefits you could imagine. That included a beautiful wife. But she was more attracted to Joseph than to her husband.

While your Bible doesn't include a photograph of Joseph, it does say that he was well-built and handsome (39:6). It also says that Joseph was one of the strongest men who ever lived. Well, it doesn't say those exact words, but it does state that he resisted the sexual advances of Potiphar's beautiful wife. That must have taken moral and physical strength because she tried to lure him every day. She even stripped the cloak off his back in an attempt to get him into her bed.

Finally Potiphar's wife retaliated against Joseph for spurning her advances. She falsely accused him of attempted rape, and Potiphar threw Joseph into jail. Under these circumstances, Joseph knew that his chances of release were about the same as if someone had thrown the cell key into the Nile.

Making Important Contacts in Jail

Things were looking pretty grim for Joseph in jail. But remember that Genesis isn't so much about the people as it is about God. And God loves to work in situations that look bleak to everyone else. So God helped Joseph make a name for himself in jail by interpreting the dreams of two of the other prisoners. Both had been on Pharaoh's staff, one as the cupbearer and the other as chief baker. Joseph interpreted their respective dreams to mean that the cupbearer would be given his job back and that the baker would be executed. Only a few days later, Joseph's interpretations proved to be right (dead right in the case of the baker).

Time Doesn't Fly When You Aren't Having Fun

The Bible is filled with examples that God's timetable is different from ours. If you were writing the story of Joseph, or if you were living his life, you would probably expect to be released from jail at the earliest possible instance. Perhaps you would expect that the cupbearer would show his appreciation by exercising his influence with Pharaoh on your behalf. But that wasn't God's timetable.

Joseph sat in jail for another two years after the cup-bearer was back in the palace. Joseph must have abandoned all hope that the cupbearer would come to his rescue. But Joseph apparently didn't abandon hope in God.

How about you? Are you willing to wait for God's timetable? Can you sit out your unpleasant circumstances until just the right moment that only God knows?

Bad dreams must have been a common malady in ancient Egypt. The same affliction befell the Pharaoh. But his dreams were so mysterious that no one could interpret them for him. God prompted Pharaoh's cupbearer to remember the young Hebrew man who had correctly interpreted the dreams of the cupbearer and the baker. Pharaoh had Joseph released from the dungeon and brought to the palace. Claiming that God would give him the power to interpret the dreams, Joseph listened as Pharaoh described what he had seen in his dreams. Joseph not only explained the meaning of the dreams but he also gave Pharaoh some recommendations for what to do:

- Egypt would enjoy seven years of unprecedented agricultural prosperity. Seven years of harsh famine would follow.

- Pharaoh should put a wise man in charge of storing up the excess during the first seven years to make grain available during the bleak seven-year famine.

Pharaoh was no fool. When you appoint a chief administrator, pick someone who has God on his side. Pharaoh immediately appointed Joseph to be in charge of all of the commerce of Egypt. God promoted Joseph from prisoner to second-in-command of Egypt in the time it took to tell and interpret a few dreams.

And God sent seven years of prosperity followed by a famine, just as Joseph had predicted.

Don't Be Cellfish

Joseph must have had a sense of God's control over his life even when he was in a jail cell. He had a positive attitude, and the head jailer had given him responsibilities. If Joseph had been self-centered and despondent, he wouldn't have been attentive to the distress of the cupbearer and the baker. He would have missed the opportunity to interpret their dreams, and the cupbearer never would have mentioned him to Pharaoh.

What lesson can you learn from all of this? What is your attitude when God puts you in circumstances that are far from desirable? Do you have a sense of God's control over your life? Do you spend all of your time thinking about yourself, or do you have enough confidence in God to focus on others?

Let's Go to Egypt for Some Take-Out

Meanwhile, back in Canaan, the future of agriculture is looking kind of grim, and the family of Jacob is looking rather thin. The famine hit all of Canaan very hard. The only way that the Jacob clan could survive was to find food in Egypt. God made sure that they heard about some administrative guru in Pharaoh's palace had stockpiled plenty of grain and that the Egyptians had food to spare.

Jacob's sons traveled to Egypt to beg for food. God directed them to Joseph. Although Joseph recognized them, they didn't know who he was. After all, they had last seen him about 20 years earlier. He was dressed as an Egyptian, and he spoke to them through an interpreter. In chapters 42–44 of Genesis, you'll read how Joseph made his brothers squirm and grovel a bit over the course of two trips to Egypt. His tactics included some false accusations of spying and theft. This wasn't done out of retaliation but rather to reveal some important information:

- The brothers felt remorse for what they had done to their brother Joseph so many years earlier (42:21-22).

- They put their own lives on the line to protect their youngest brother, Benjamin, and the feelings of their father (44:18-34).

The change in his brothers that had occurred over the previous two decades moved and impressed Joseph. He revealed his identity, and the brothers enjoyed a big celebration. But the family reunion wasn't complete just yet. Joseph made arrangements for his father to permanently move down to Egypt, where the entire family of Jacob settled.

On Jacob's death, Joseph arranged for a burial in Canaan according to his father's wishes. Joseph's brothers then worried that Joseph had been holding a grudge against them but was refraining from retaliation while their father was alive. With Jacob dead, Joseph might use his powerful position in Egypt to have them jailed or killed. But Joseph reassured them with his perspective on God's providence and provision:

> Don't be afraid of me. Am I God, to judge and punish you? As far as I am concerned, God turned into good what you meant for evil. He brought me to the high position I have today so I could save the lives of many people (Genesis 50:19-20).

Joseph knew that God had directed each of the events of his life.

Joseph lived with his brothers and their families in Egypt for about 75 years. Before he died at the age of 110, he reiterated the plan that God made in the covenant to great-grandfather Abraham:

> *"Soon I will die," Joseph told his brothers, "but God will surely come for you, to lead you out of this land of Egypt. He will bring you back to the land he vowed to give to the descendants of Abraham, Isaac, and Jacob"* (Genesis 50:24).

Perhaps more than his brothers, father, grandfather, or great-grandfather, Joseph had a grasp of God's protection and provision. He understood the significance of the covenant and God's ability to work the circumstances of the world around the fulfillment of it.

When you get to the book of Exodus, you learn that the descendants of Jacob lived in Egypt for 400 years (they became the slaves of the Egyptians until Moses led them out of captivity). This extended detour to Egypt was no mere coincidence. It was the fulfillment of what God promised when He told Abraham that his descendants would live in Egypt for 400 years before returning to the Promised Land (Genesis 15:13).

◻ ◻ ◻

Study the Word

1. The Old Testament refers to dreams primarily when God speaks to an individual (see Genesis 20:3; 31:10-11; 31:24, Numbers 12:6 and Job 33:14-15). Occasionally, dreams mentioned in the Old Testament have an element of foretelling future events (see Daniel, chapters 2 and 7). But we must be careful that

we don't place undue importance on dreams. What instruction does the Bible give in this regard in Jeremiah 23:28 and Deuteronomy 13:1-4?

2. Review the generosity that Pharaoh showed to Joseph's family as reported in Genesis 45:16-20. What does this tell you about the impression that Joseph made on his employer? Nehemiah is another example of a God-fearing man who won favor with a pagan king. Read about his request for a favor from King Artexerxes in Nehemiah 1:1–2:8. What do the examples of Joseph and Nehemiah suggest to you about being an effective witness for Christ in the workplace?

3. Reread Genesis 43. Describe the character and feelings of Jacob, Judah, and Joseph based on what each man did.

4. Retrace the events (and injustices) in Joseph's life. How did each circumstance help prepare him for his future? What might have been the progression of his character development? How would his life story be helpful if you were counseling someone who had experienced injustice in their life circumstances? How can God's continued protection of Joseph encourage you about your present situation?

Dig Deeper

We hope that you'll want to go further in your study of Genesis. Here are some additional resources that may be of help to you.

Commentaries

Paradise to Prison—Studies in Genesis by John J. Davis is not your ordinary commentary. It is written more as a narrative than a verse-by-verse explanation.

Check out the *Genesis* volume by Howard F. Vos in the Everyman's Bible Commentary series. This book takes a one-passage-at-a-time approach. The explanations of Bible background are very helpful.

Derek Kidner wrote the *Genesis* volume of the Tyndale Old Testament Commentaries. You'll find solid information in this book, but it is in the traditional examination of one word at a time.

Sometimes the commentaries we used weren't just on Genesis but covered the entire Old Testament. That is the case with The Old Testament volume of *The Bible Knowledge Commentary,* edited by John Walvoord and Roy Zuck.

If you want to understand Genesis as part of the whole sweep of history, you may want to read *Bible History—Old Testament* by Alfred Edersheim. Our copy has over 1000 pages, but the Genesis portion is covered in about the first 130 pages.

We have in our libraries two other single-volume commentaries on the whole Bible: The *Matthew Henry Commentary* and *The Wycliffe Bible Commentary.* Our copies are well-worn (and that's not because we bought them used).

General Bible Study Helps

Modesty prohibits us from suggesting our own *Knowing the Bible 101.* It is a great user-friendly resource, but you didn't hear that from us.

We hope you are experiencing the rewards of studying the Bible. If you are ready to be a real student of the Word, then you might want to read *How to Study Your Bible* by Kay Arthur. Get your colored pencils ready because you'll be using them if you follow Kay's disciplined approach.

Speaking of being a student, sometimes a "survey" course is helpful for a general overview. We like the textbook, *An Introduction to the Old Testament,* written by Raymond B. Dillard and our friend, Tremper Longman III. This book can give you an overall perspective.

Bible Translations

Lots of translations of the Bible are available to you. We suggest that your primary study Bible be a *literal* translation (as opposed to a paraphrase), such as the *New International Version* (NIV) of the Bible or the *New American Standard Bible* (NASB). However, using a Bible paraphrase such as *The Living Bible* or *The Message* in your devotional reading is perfectly acceptable.

In this book we have been using the *New Living Translation* (NLT), a Bible translation that uses a method called "dynamic equivalence." This means that the scholars who translated the Bible from the original languages (Hebrew and Greek) used a "thought-for-thought" translation philosophy rather than a "word-for-word" approach. It's just as accurate but easier to read. In the final analysis, the Bible that's best for you is the Bible you enjoy reading because you can understand it.

A Word About Personal Pronouns

Did you notice that we prefer to capitalize all personal pronouns that refer to God, Jesus, and the Holy Spirit (such as *He, Him,* and *His*)? Some writers don't. We do—it's just a matter of personal preference. In fact, personal pronouns for God were not capitalized in the original languages, which is why you'll find that the Bible uses *he, him, his,* and *himself.* We do it in symbolic reverence and to remind ourselves how big God is and how small we are.

Bruce and Stan would enjoy hearing from you.
The best ways to contact them are...

Snail mail: Twelve Two Media,
PO Box 25597
Fresno, CA 93729-5597

E-mail: info@twelvetwomedia.com

Web site: www.twelvetwomedia.com

Christianity 101™ Bible Studies

Genesis: Discovering God's Answers to Life's Ultimate Questions
What did God have in mind when He started this world? What happened to His perfect design? Join Bruce and Stan in this exciting survey and learn how God's record of ancient times impacts *our* time.

Ephesians: Finding Your Identity in Christ
This inviting little guide to the book of Ephesians gets straight to the heart of Paul's teaching on the believer's identity in Christ: We belong to Christ, the Holy Spirit is our guarantee, and we can share in God's power.

John: Encountering Christ in a Life-Changing Way
John records how Jesus changed the lives of everyone He met. Bruce and Stan's fresh approach to these narratives will help you have your own personal, life-changing encounter with Jesus, the Son of God.

Revelation: Unlocking the Mysteries of the End Times
Just what is really going to happen? In this fascinating look at the apostle John's prophecy, Bruce and Stan demonstrate why—when God's involved—the end of the world is something to look forward to.

Exclusive Online Feature

Here's a Bible study feature you're really going to like!
Simply go online at:

www.christianity101online.com

There you'll find a website designed exclusively for users of the Christianity 101 Bible Studies series. When you log on to the site, just click on the book you are studying, and you will discover additional information, resources, and helps, including...

- *Background Material*—We can't put everything in this Bible study, so this online section includes more material, such as historical, geographical, theological, and biographical information.

- *More Questions*—Do you need more questions for your Bible study? Here are additional questions for each chapter. Bible study leaders will find this especially helpful.

- *Answers to Your Questions*—Do you have a question about something in your Bible study? Post your question and an "online scholar" will respond.

- *FAQs*—In this section are answers to some of the more frequently asked questions about the book you are studying.

What are you waiting for? Go online and become a part of the Christianity 101 community!

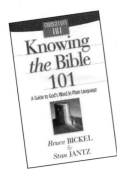

Knowing the Bible 101
A fresh approach to making Christianity understandable—even the hard parts! This user-friendly book relies on humor, insights, and relevant examples that will inspire readers not only to make sense of Scripture, but to *enjoy* Bible study.

Bruce & Stan's® *Guide Series:*

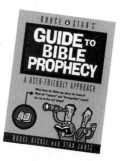

Bruce & Stan's® Guide to Bible Prophecy
Dealing with prophecy and end times in their witty, down-to-earth way, Bruce and Stan offer the Bible's answers to readers' big questions. Is the end really near? Who is the Antichrist? What is the Rapture?

Bruce & Stan's® Guide to Cults, Religions, and Spiritual Beliefs
"Here is our purpose, plain and simple: to provide an understandable overview of predominant religions and spiritual beliefs (with a little sense of humor thrown in along the way)." Clear explanations help readers understand the core issues of more than a dozen religions.

Bruce & Stan's® Guide to God
This fresh, user-friendly guide to the Christian life is designed to help new believers get started or recharge the batteries of believers of any age. Humorous subtitles, memorable icons, and learning aids present even difficult concepts in a simple way. Perfect for personal use or group study.

Bruce & Stan's® Pocket Guide Series:

· ·

Available from Harvest House Publishers:

Bruce & Stan's® Pocket Guide to Prayer
This very portable guide to prayer is as fun to read as it is uplifting. Readers will experience the wonder of communicating directly with God as Bruce and Stan explore the truth about how and why to pray.

Bruce & Stan's® Pocket Guide to Islam
Cutting through the mystery of Islam, Bruce and Stan's look at the world's second largest religion will help Christians better understand and witness to Muslims. Includes information about the Koran and Muslims' beliefs about Christ.

· ·

Available from Twelve Two Media:

To order these Pocket Guides,
visit www.twelvetwomedia.com

Bruce & Stan's® Pocket Guide to Knowing God's Will
Here, the wise and witty Bruce and Stan help readers discover the practical realities of hearing God, discerning His will, and walking in His perfect plan. Easy-to-understand explanations, highlighted with eye-catching graphics.

Bruce & Stan's® Pocket Guide to Knowing the Holy Spirit
The Holy Spirit often seems a most mysterious person. Bruce and Stan explore the many dimensions of His role in our lives. Covers "quenching the Spirit" and how to avoid it, and helpful ways to hear the Holy Spirit's voice.

Bruce & Stan's® Pocket Guide to Knowing Jesus
Using charts, sidebars, and information icons, this concise guide answers questions about Jesus and clarifies misconceptions about salvation, faith, and grace. Addresses the "all God, all-man" mystery, and the amazing truth of Christ's resurrection.

Bruce & Stan's® Pocket Guide to Sharing Your Faith
Great graphics and clear explanations make this guide easy to use. Readers will discover practical insights and ideas for confirming their own faith, handling objections about God and the Bible, and leading people to Jesus.

Bruce & Stan's® Pocket Guide to Studying Your Bible
Bruce and Stan cut through difficult concepts, unfamiliar customs and awkward names to make Bible study accessible and fun. Readers will explore Bible organization, translation differences, and effective ways to apply God's truths.